MASTERING

COMPUTER PRO

C000104445

MACMILLAN MASTER SERIES

Accounting
Arabic
Astronomy
Australian History
Background to Business
Banking
Basic Management
Biology
British Politics
Business Communication
Business Law
Business Microcomputing
Catering Science
Catering Theory
Chemistry
COBOL Programming
Commerce
Computer Programming
Computers
Economic and Social History
Economics
Electrical Engineering
Electronics
English as a Foreign Language
English Grammar
English Language
English Literature
Financial Accounting
French 1
French 2

German 1
German 2
Hairdressing
Italian 1
Italian 2
Japanese
Keyboarding
Marketing
Mathematics
Modern British History
Modern European History
Modern World History
Nutrition
Office Practice
Pascal Programming
Philosophy
Physics
Practical Writing
Principles of Accounts
Restaurant Service
Social Welfare
Sociology
Spanish 1
Spanish 2
Spreadsheets
Statistics
Statistics with your Microcomputer
Study Skills
Typewriting Skills
Word Processing

MASTERING
COMPUTER PROGRAMMING

THIRD EDITION

P. E. GOSLING

MACMILLAN

First edition 1982
Reprinted 1982, 1983
Second edition 1984
Reprinted 1985
Third edition 1990
Reprinted 1990

Published by
MACMILLAN EDUCATION LTD
Houndmills, Basingstoke, Hampshire RG21 2XS
and London
Companies and representatives
throughout the world

Printed in Great Britain by
Billing and Sons Ltd
Worcester

British Library Cataloguing in Publication Data
Gosling, P. E. (Peter Edward)
Mastering computer programming.—(3rd ed.).
1. Computer systems. Programming languages: Basic
language
I. Title   II. Series
005.13'3
ISBN 0–333–51005–4 Pbk
ISBN 0–333–51006–2 Pbk export

CONTENTS

PREFACE

Despite the fact that so many specialised "packages" have come onto the market since the first edition of this book was published in 1982 there is still a need for people to learn the art of programming. Many of these packages possess their own internal programming facility ofen cloaked under the name of a *macro*. Even the WordPerfect word processing program, on which this book was written, has a powerful programming language available. The macro facility in the Lotus 1–2–3 and SuperCalc spreadsheets enable you to do things with them that one would never have dreamed of in the days when all spreadsheets did was to update stock lists and perform complex calculations at great speed. You can see how these macros are created in my book *Mastering Spreadsheets*.

So this book is intended to be a guided tour of programming and what it involves. Its object, as with the previous two editions, is to introduce the techniques of writing computer programs. The reader should realise that the first step in writing a program is that is should be *planned* carefully. The most important part of programming is the *method* that is adopted to achieve the required end. The rest is then to decide which *language* is best suited to the job in hand and finally the end of the task is to *code* the program in that language. As you will see, you would not use a language such as PROLOG to perform mathematical calculations, nor would you use C for handling files of numerical data. "Horses for Courses" is the watchword in programming.

In the preparation of this book I must extend my grateful thanks to Lauretta Hooper of Keene Business to Business for supplying me with the latest versions of Borland International's Turbo Pascal, Turbo C and Turbo PROLOG. My colleague Frank Hatfull has been of great service as well in offering help and suggestions together with a program that I would never have dreamed of writing myself.

I have tried to produce as many varied examples as possible; I hope that we have a sort of "Hitch-hiker's Guide to Programming" so that the reader will gain the flavour of the various programming languages dealt with. This book in no way attempts to give detailed descriptions, which is why the reader is pointed in the direction of more comprehensive texts (see Further Reading) in order to gain an in-depth understanding of a particular language.

The important thing about programming is that it requires *practice*. It is very much a "doing" activity and reading all the books in the world will not make a competent programmer. You will only learn by your mistakes, as the author well knows in the preparation of the examples for this book. Remember the golden rules

NO PROGRAM OF OVER FOUR LINES EVER WORKS FIRST TIME

DON'T PANIC

DON'T GIVE UP

February 1989   Peter Gosling

GLOSSARY
OF TRADEMARKS

dBASE	Ashton-Tate Compnay
dBASE III PLUS	Ashton-Tate Company
GWBASIC	MicroSoft Corporation
MS-DOS	MicroSoft Corporation
Turbo Pascal	Borland International
Turbo C	Borland International
Turbo PROLOG	Borland International

WHAT IS A COMPUTER PROGRAM?

1.1 INTRODUCTION

If one wanted to define what a computer is, then the following would probably fill the bill:

a high-speed, automatic, electronic, digital, general purpose, stored program data processing machine.

It is not the purpose of this book to cover every aspect of this definition. In fact, the only part which really concerns us is the *stored program* concept. However, it is because a computer is electronic and high-speed that it is able to use a stored program in order to process data very quickly. In other words, there are pieces of electronics which constitute the memory inside the computer which are able to store a sequence of instructions, permanently if need be. These instructions can be brought into operation automatically in order to process the data which is presented to them. The concept of a computer being a device which produces the answers to a series of questions is very over-simplified and a rather romantic idea of what a computer really is, thanks to television and the popular press!

The concept of a computer program becomes easier to understand if we look at a computer as a kind of *electronic filing cabinet*. Let us take an example to illustrate the way in which data can be processed by such a machine. Consider a case where a computer is used to keep track of the amount of stock held in the stores of a factory. First of all we need a list of all the stock items *currently held* in the stores. This list will contain information, usually in part number order, about the number of each item of stock, its description, its cost, the minimum reorder level and so on. All this information will be stored in the computer's memory on magnetic disks on what is generally called a *file*. If all the information about the movement of stock, also in part number order, is placed on another file on the disk then a program of instructions, stored in yet another part of the memory, is brought into action. This program will cause the information stored in the movements file to be merged with the current stock file so that a new, up-to-date, stock file is created. If all the data had been written down on pieces of paper then a clerk would have to have made the amendments by hand in a ledger - which is another name for a file. This job is very boring, repetitive and error-prone. In fact it is exactly the kind of job computers are good at. Because computers never get bored and they are unlikely - again despite what the media say - to make mistakes, they are ideal for taking over these boring, repetitive tasks. People make mistakes; computers do not unless there is a malfunction in the electronics. TV and radio sets rarely go wrong so there is little chance, given proper maintenance, that a computer should actually fail to work properly. After all, how many times do you tune a TV set to BBC 2 and get Channel 4? But that is the kind of "mistake" a computer is supposed to make. If a computer program is used to perform routine tasks they will be performed as fast and as efficiently as the design of the computer *hardware* and the computer program, the *software*, will allow. If a further job has to be carried out on our stock file, such as scanning it to detect any stock levels below the reorder level and printing the necessary orders, another program needs to be called into action. *One* program is used for *one* job.

The whole attitude to programming can be summed up simply in the words of a student the author once taught. After about four weeks of a programming course the student suddenly said, "I realise now that you need to know how to solve your problem before giving it to the computer!"

It is not difficult to see how raw data, which can consist only of numbers and/or names, can be stored. All that is needed is some code which enables alphabetic and numeric characters to be stored electronically.

1.2 THE USER AS PROGRAMMER

When the first edition of this book was written the use of the Personal Computer (PC, which now refers to any IBM compatible micro-computer) was nothing like as widespread as it is now. Seven years of growth in the PC market has placed machines of this type not only within the reach of even the smallest businesses but also onto the desk of the majority of managers. Where once upon a time there were computer users, computer operators and computer programmers as three separate and distinct groups the PC user has to perform the functions of all three in many cases. This is partly to do with the fact that there are so many incredibly sophisticated programs on the market for the PC at reasonable prices. Many of these programs, particularly the database and spreadsheet programs, are "solutions looking for a problem to solve" and if you examine these at just below the trivial level you will see that to get the best out of them you need to be able to perform a programming function yourself. A good example of this is the dBASE™ programming language which is dealt with in Chapter 10 of this book. This is one of the languages that has become much used since the first edition of this book was written. Another is the language of artificial intelligence, PROLOG. Now that so-called "Expert" systems are becoming used more and more people who use computers often need to produce their own systems. It is for this reason that a chapter on the PROLOG language has been included. The old favourites of BASIC, COBOL and Pascal have been retained in this edition and a chapter on the new "programmers'" language, called simply C, has been included. The author also decided not to pursue any further study of FORTRAN as this is still very much the province of the scientific programmer and not in such common use on PCs.

1.3 PLANNING YOUR PROGRAM

There has always been a confusion in the minds of students between *programming* and *coding*. The first of these terms is used to describe the logical steps made in the solving of a problem: what the author's student meant when he said that he had to know how to solve the problem himself before handing it over to the computer. Once this series of steps has been established then a decision can be made regarding how these steps can be translated into the instructions used by a particular computer language. Each computer language has its own features that make it suitable for the solution of certain types of problems. COBOL, for example is very good for handling files of data and manipulating that data. The dBASE™ programming language is fine for handling large databases and extracting information from them. Neither of these are particularly good at performing complex arithmetic calculations, there are other programming languages that are far better. So before one begins actually to write a program the thoughts about it have to go on paper in some sort of a plan. Now there are basically two ways in which this can be accomplished. The first, and more traditional method is to draw a *flow chart* to show the steps taken to solve the problem in the form of a diagram. First of all, the problem:

> The electricity company makes a standing charge of £3.25 on all bills and there is a minimum charge of £3.64 for electricity consumed in addition to the standing charge. The first 150 units are charged at 7p per unit and all units used over 150 are charged at the reduced rate of 5p per unit. VAT at 15% is charged on all bills.

What is needed is some method of threading one's way through a series of steps, starting with the knowledge of the number of units used, to emerge at the other end with a final figure owing to the electricity company. This can be expressed in words something like this:

> **The number of units used must be tested to see if it is less than or equal to 150. If it is then the number of units is multiplied by .07 to give the basic cost in pounds. The number obtained must then be tested to see if it is less than 3.64. If it is then the basic cost is set to be 3.64. 3.25 is added onto the basic cost. Then the total including VAT at 15% is calculated and the answer displayed. If the number of units exceeded 150 then the number of units above 150 is calculated and multiplied by .05. This figure is added to 10.5 (the cost of 150 units at .07) and then the final cost including VAT is calculated and displayed.**

As a piece of prose the above is tortuous and difficult to understand; it can be expressed in chart form giving a far clearer idea of how the final answer is arrived at. This chart is shown in Fig. 1.1

As an alternative way of describing the process you could state it in what is known as a *structured* form. In this the steps are described in a way that you could easily explain to someone over a telephone, which is far easier in fact than explaining a flow chart to someone by the same method! The sequence of events is broken down, in this case into sixteen steps. You should notice that no account is taken of the fact that the program is dealing with units of electricity and amounts of money. These are all numbers and it is only we who know that they must have some units attached to them.

Fig 1.1 *A simple flow chart*

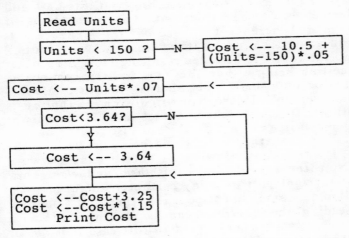

1. Read units
2. If units <= 150
3.   Then
4.   Set Cost:=units*.07
5.   Else
6.   Set Cost:=10.5+(units-150)*.05
7. Ifend
8. If Cost<3.64
9.   Then
10.   Set Cost:=3.64
11.   Else
12.   Skip
13. Ifend
14. Set Cost:=(Cost+3.25)*1.15
15. Print Cost
16. End

Read the above instructions out loud and you will see that it makes sense.

In both of these examples you can see that there are two main kinds of instruction written down. One is what is often called an *assignment* statement where, for example "Cost <-- Cost+3.25" means "increase the cost by 3.25". In the structured example (on p. 5) the term "Set Cost:=Cost+3.25" has exactly the same meaning. You should notice that := or <-- are used rather than an = sign. This is because what you have written is not a statement of fact but an *instruction*. It is very easy to write "Cost = Cost+3.25" and not realise exactly what is meant. The other kind of instruction used here is the *decision test*. The test is enclosed in a box from which there are only two ways out. These give the routes to be taken resulting from the answer to the question being either "Yes" or "No". In computing, questions can only have one of two answers. "Maybe" cannot be acceptable. In the structured example the test is posed within a structure that in effect says "If the answer to this question is Yes <u>then</u> do this, or <u>else</u> (if the answer is not Yes) do that, the whole thing being started by the keyword "If" and finished with the terminating keyword "Ifend". Note the use of the words *then* and *else*. They form an important part of many computer languages.

The only other things to notice is that there must be some way of "seeding" the procedure, that is, starting it off with some data. The word usually used in this case is *input* or *read*. In this case it is a single number representing the number of units used. You will see later that computer programs can manipulate characters as well as numbers. The other thing is an instruction to output, or display, an answer. Everything a computer has to do must be clearly and unambiguously defined for it. It is just as if you were telling some totally ignorant person how to change a light bulb. You must not leave any step out or assume that it will be done without any further instructions.

1.4 STORING DATA IN MEMORY

Once one understands the basic workings of a computer then the concept of the storage of data is quite simple to follow - for further details you could refer to *Mastering Computers* by G.G.L.Wright. The majority of computers, whether mainframe, mini or micro (and now the dividing lines are becoming more and more blurred), are designed around the concept of the computer *word*. A "word" is the basic unit of information used by a computer and is a collection of *bits* (*bi*nary dig*its*) and contains 8, 16 or 32 bits as a rule. Eight bits are collectively known as one *byte* and if we stick to the byte concept we shall be able to follow the descriptions of data storage used in this and subsequent chapters. Basically, a computer can store three types of data: *integer* numbers, *floating point* numbers and *characters*. An integer, a whole number, can be either positive or negative and needs two bytes of storage, that is, one word of a PC's memory. A floating point number, one which contains a decimal part as well as an integer part, needs four bytes of storage, that is if it is to contain a maximum of six significant digits. If more storage is required for a floating point number then its number of significant digits is increased. If six significant digits are stored then the number is said to be stored with *single precision*. A character, which can be any letter of the alphabet, the digits 0 through 9 and special characters such as @, %, +, =, &, etc., need one byte of storage so that one sixteen bit word in a PC's memory can store two characters. The codes allocated to characters are according to the ASCII convention (American Standard Code for Information Interchange, pronounced "ASKEY").

The version of BASIC available on most PCs allows a distinction to be made between single and double precision floating point numbers, with a considerable increase in the accuracy of the arithmetic they can perform. The distinction between the use of integers and floating point numbers may not be easy to grasp initially but suffice it to say that we should always do our counting using integers and our arithmetic using floating point numbers.

During the running of any computer program areas of memory have to be allocated to each *variable* used in the program. In our electricity bill program there are two variables: *units* and *cost*. These will actually refer to specific memory locations in the RAM (**R**andom **A**ccess **M**emory) of the PC. In the early days of computer programming we had to refer to memory locations by number and in very long programs this became a nightmare trying to remember which location was which. Nowadays we are able to refer to the locations by name and let the computer software take care of allocating specific locations to the names.

1.5 DISK STORAGE

The disks which every PC has are used as bulk storage media and are used for the storage of files of data. Programs are stored on disk and files of information are stored on disk as well. The computer makes no discrimination between these. It is only us and our programming skill that does. You should remember that when a program is executed, or "run" then it can only run once it has been loaded into RAM. This means that while a program is running this memory is being used for *two* tasks. One of these is the storage of the program, whose instructions are executed one at a time in sequence, and the other is the temporary storage of data while the program is running. Whatever happens in RAM is of a transient nature and will disappear once a new program is executed or if the machine is switched off. Data stored on disk is permanent, or as permanent as anything recorded magnetically can be. This means that such things as stock files, lists of names and addresses and bank transactions are there for all time until some program comes along and modifies or deletes them. The same thing goes for computer programs. They are created, simply by typing them in under certain conditions, and then recorded onto disk ready for use. The disks commonly used will be, if removable, capable of storing from 360k bytes (approximately 360,000 characters) to 1.4M bytes (1,440,000 characters approximately). If fixed, or hard, disks are used then they are capable of storing anything from 10M bytes (10,000,000 characters approximately) upwards of data. A 20M byte disk is perfectly capable of holding a large number of programs and enough data to run a small business.

1.6 SERIAL AND RANDOM FILES

A file of data is used in exactly the same way as a set of index cards or the pages of a ledger. If you had a set of names and addresses arranged in alphabetical order of surnames that you wanted to use to produce a series of letters, each individually addressed, then you would proceed through this list in order from beginning to end until the job was complete. If, on the other hand, you had a stock file and you wished to add some new stock onto one particular item you would not start at the beginning of that list and systematically work through it in order to find the one you wanted; if that one was the last one you would not want to read through every single record in that file until you arrived at the one you wanted. You would want some way of getting to that record as quickly as possible without reading through unnecessary records. Such a technique is known as *random file accessing*. It is used all the time in, for example, a cash dispenser. The program that drives the cash dispenser must have some means of finding your account number from among the millions of others there are. If it did not then the queues outside these machines would be even longer than they are at present. How to make use of these techniques will be dealt with in Chapter 5.

1.7 SORTING

One of the most boring jobs you can be called upon to do is to sort papers into order. There are many ways, as you will see, for computers to make the sorting process fast and efficient. One of the most difficult tasks to give a novice to programming is to ask him to write a program to sort three numbers into order. The author well remembers trying this for the first time and the program being of inordinate length. Eventually it became refined down to five simple instructions. Sorting will be dealt with in Chapter 4.

1.8 HANDLING CHARACTERS

It has already been said that computer programs have to be able to manipulate characters. After all, that is what a word processor program does all the time - see *Mastering Word Processing* (2nd edn) by Peter and Joanna Gosling. In the type of program you will have described in this book you will see that characters are easily dealt with. They are usually known as "strings", and your program must be able to differentiate between, for example, the number **126** and the string of characters "**126**". As was described earlier in this chapter, these are stored in totally different ways. If you try to perform arithmetic on characters you obtain some very strange answers. Although **126 + 10** gives us **136**, "**126**" + "**10**" gives "**12610**". It is a process called *concatenation*, where one string is appended onto the end of another. Sets of characters can be sorted in the same way as sets of numbers and in fact mixed sets of strings of alphabetical and numerical characters can be sorted because there is a precedence of numerical characters over alphabetical characters. Character handling is dealt with in Chapter 4.

CHAPTER 2

BASIC:

A POPULAR LANGUAGE

2.1 INTRODUCTION

For a large part of this book the language called BASIC
(Beginner's Allpurpose Symbolic Instruction Code) is going
to be used to introduce the most important aspects of
programming. This is not a book about programming in
BASIC, but it is a book about programming and some of
the techniques required to write good computer programs.
To find out the details of writing programs in BASIC, or
any other of the languages available, the reader should
consult either the programming manuals issued by the
computer companies or books devoted to the specific
language which is chosen to be studied in depth. There are
a number of versions of BASIC available today and the one
used for the examples in this book is the one known as
GWBASIC, the *GW* standing for *Gee Whizz*! This language
is often supplied free when you purchase the MS-DOS™
operating system.

All computer languages need instructions which will
cause a specific set of computer operations to take place.
With a high level language such as BASIC one statement
can generate a large number of the simple machine
instructions that actually are carried out by the
microprocessor chip. The instructions that a high-level
language needs to provide will:

(1)   Control the input of data to, and the output of
        data from, the computer's memory. These are
        usually called *input/output* (I/O) instructions.

(2)   Cause the computer to perform arithmetic
        operations. These are usually called *assignment*
        instructions since they cause arithmetic to take

place and assign the results to specific locations in memory.

(3)   Tell the computer how the data it is processing should be stored. (This may not make a lot of sense at the moment but soon you will see that it is important that data is stored in different forms.)

(4)   Allow logical decisions to be made; these are called *conditional jump* instructions.

(5)   Control the *order* in which the set of instructions which make up the program are executed.

A computer program has to start somewhere, usually as a problem to be solved, and the first step in writing a program is to decide, in outline at least, how the problem is to be tackled. We have already looked at this briefly in Chapter 1, but there you were presented with the finished article. Later on in this book, in Chapter 8, we will look at this process in more detail. At this stage we will look at the simple task of totalling up a shopping list. The data which is needed occurs in the form of pairs of numbers. These numbers represent how many of each item is bought and the amount paid for each of them. The output from the program would be the total cost of the goods bought. But the computer is not interested in the fact that it was three tins of baked beans that were bought at 24 pence each, only that it has to perform certain manipulations on the numbers 3 and 24. Only the programmer knows, or cares, that the numbers represent tins and amounts of money. So far, so good. The solution to the problem falls into several phases. The first of these is the phase in which the computer is supplied with a set of pairs of numbers representing, in order, the cost in pounds and the number purchased of each. The pairs of numbers would be, say

    1.41, 1, 0.66, 2, 1.78, 1, 0.24, 3, . . .

meaning that there was one item bought for £1.41, two at 66p, one at £1.78, three at 24p and so on. To total the bill we need to multiply the pairs of numbers together and add the answer into a running total for the bill until we reach the end of the list of goods purchased. This all implies that the data, which is the set of pairs of numbers, has to be placed in the computer's memory, and a multiplication sum performed on each pair of numbers; the answer is then added to the running total, which is also held in the computer's memory. When the input of data comes to an end another part of the program has to be executed so that the final total is printed out. Then the program will stop. This means that the computer must in some way know that the input list has come to an end so that the repeated operation of multiplication and addition into the total ceases and the loop is broken out of before the final total is displayed. Therefore there must be some mechanism which is constantly asking, "Have we come to the end of the list?" If the answer is "Yes" then the final stages of the program are executed. If the answer is "No" then the loop in which the two numbers are input, their product calculated and the answer added into the total is carried out yet again. Luckily computers never get tired of asking the same question and then carrying out the same old boring calculation if the answer to the question tells them that it must be done again, even if it is for the millionth time. This is, of course, in direct contrast to the parent who, 100 yards from home on a car journey, is asked by a child, "Are we there yet?"

The BASIC instructions that signal the various types of operation to the computer are dealt with in this and the next five chapters. How other languages handle them is described in Chapters 8-14.

2.2 BASIC

You may have noticed that computers operate on both *variables*, whose values are not known at the time when the program is written, and *constants,* which are numbers supplied by the program itself. A good example of this is the electricity bill program in Chapter 1, where the number of units is input by the person running the program. The number of units will be a variable, as indeed will be the cost which is calculated according to the number of units used. The constants are the numbers which represent the cost per unit, standing charges, VAT rate and so on.

In most versions of BASIC the variables are referred to be letters of the alphabet, or a letter followed by a single digit, for example, A, K, X1, H7, and so on. In GWBASIC, and a number of other variants of the language, you are allowed to use words to refer to variables, for example Cost, Units, etc. These are known officially as *Symbolic Addresses*, because although we do not know the precise location of the variable in RAM the computer software has allocated it for us. The only pitfall here is that you must not use certain "reserved words" for variable names. BASIC uses these for special purposes. So variable names such as **WIDTH**, **NEXT** or **LINE** are out.

BASIC uses *assignment* statements that look like this:

LET P = Q + R - 4

or

LET COST = PRICE * NUMBER

The first of these statements means that the variable **Q** contains a number that must be added to the value of the variable stored in **R** and the constant **4** must be subtracted from their sum and the answer assigned to the variable **P**. Similarly the second statement means that the variable stored in **COST** is assigned the product of the variable stored in **PRICE** and the variable stored in **NUMBER**. Whatever we may choose to call the variables we use, the microprocessor will have assigned specific numbered locations to these names, which, generally speaking, we need know nothing about as all this is "transparent" to us. The word **LET** is optional in most versions of BASIC but it is very useful for the novice to use since the = sign in an assignment statement is not used in the conventional mathematical way. In BASIC the = sign is used to stand for the "takes the value of". There can only be one variable name on the left-hand side of the assignment statement so that the assignment operation consists of performing the arithmetic on the variables and constants on the right-hand side and the result of that calculation assigned to the variable name on the left-hand side.

Constants in BASIC can be positive or negative decimal numbers with or without a sign preceding them. The absence of a sign implies that the number is positive. Very large or very small numbers can be written in a special standard form which is of the following structure

dEe

where **d** is a decimal number and **e** is a power of 10 so that

3497.973

can be written as

3.497973E3

which stands for

$$3.497973 \times 10^3$$

The letter **E** (for Exponent, stands for "times 10 to the power of". Similarly the number

0.000005697

can be written as

5.e-6

standing for

$$5.697 \times 10^{-6}$$

In addition, the number

-0.0010203

can be written as

-1.000203E-3

Double precision numbers are automatically assumed if they contain more than seven significant digits or are written in the form

dDe

or

3.50#

Arithmetic operations in BASIC are indicated by the following symbols

+	add
-	subtract
*	multiply
/	divide
↑	exponentiate (raise to the power of)

Brackets are used to group operations together and reduce ambiguity. There is a hierarchy of arithmetic operations which bears a distinct relationship to the old-fashioned **BODMAS** (Brackets, Of, Division, Multiplication, Addition, Subtraction) rule of arithmetic. The rule in BASIC is **BEDMAS** (Brackets, Exponentiation, Division, Multiplication, Addition, Subtraction).

Any arithmetic rule in BASIC is always evaluated according to this rule. For example

$$(4 + 6)\uparrow2 + 3 * 4$$
$$= \quad 10\uparrow2 + 3 * 4$$
$$= \quad 100 + 3 * 4$$
$$= \quad 100 + 12$$
$$= \quad 112$$

The **INPUT** command means

connect the input device to memory and load whatever is typed into memory

PRINT - often shortened to **?**

means

copy the contents of specific memory location onto the output device

STOP

means stop the program.

END

is usually optional and acts in a similar manner to **STOP**. Refer to the computer manufacturer's manual to find if it is essential. Sometimes it must be the very last statement in the program.

Every BASIC instruction is prefixed by a line number and the program is always executed in line number order beginning at the lowest numbered line. A simple BASIC program is shown in Fig. 2.1 to illustrate the points just made. It accepts two numbers from your keyboard - the input device - and calculates their sum and displays it on the screen. The command **RUN** causes the program to start executing from the lowest numbered line.

Fig 2.1

```
10  INPUT A,B
20  C= A+B
30  ? C
40  STOP
RUN
? 3,4
 7
Break in 40
Ok
RUN
? 1.08E+4,-3.07E+6
-3059200
Break in 40
Ok
RUN
? -9.08786E-7,-5.6754E-8
-1.044614E-06
Break in 40
Ok
```

Program outline: The first part of Fig. 2.1 shows the program instructions which are retained in memory as they are typed in. The programmer then types RUN and the program starts executing at the first line, line number 10. Because it has the instruction INPUT to execute the computer will print a ? prompt and expect two numbers, since there are two variable names after the word INPUT. In the first instance the value 3 will be assigned to the variable A and 4 to the variable B. The program will then continue to the next line where the variables A and B are added together to assign a value to the variable C. Finally the value of the variable C is to be printed and the program will stop. Notice that the answer, 7 in this case, is printed and followed by the statement, Break in 40, which tells us that the program has reached a STOP at line 40. The program is now run twice more with different pairs of numbers. Each time the RUN command is issued the program executes from the lowest line number. On most PCs you will find that function key F2 can be pressed to set the program running.

We now know sufficient BASIC to use the language to perform simple arithmetic calculations and some examples of these are shown in Fig. 2.2. What we are doing is using the computer to *evaluate formulas* for us. The FORTRAN language was developed specifically for such operations - hence its name FORmula TRANslator.

Fig 2.2

```
10  INPUT A,B,C
20  D = B↑2 - 4*A*C
30  ? D
40  STOP

10  INPUT U,F,T
20  S = U*T + 0.5*F*T*T
30  ? S
40  STOP

10  INPUT P,T,R
20  I = P*T*R/100
30  ? I
40  STOP

10  INPUT A,B
20  X=(A+B)/(A-B)
30  ? X
40  END
```

Program outline: In each of the programs in Fig. 2.2 the first line will request numbers to be input and the ? prompt displayed. Once the appropriate number of items has been entered, three in the first three examples and two in the last one, line 20 will perform the evaluation of some formula, specified according to the rules of BASIC, and then the value of the variable specified on the left-hand side of expression in line 20 is displayed when line 30 is reached. Then the program stops.

As well as allowing us to evaluate formulas, BASIC allows us to call for such operations which would usually send us hunting in sets of tables. Such things as square roots, sines, cosines, and so on, are easily available to the BASIC programmer. All that is needed is the code **SQR** for the square root to be evaluated, like this

$$A = SQR(X)$$

where **A** is the square root of the number stored under the variable name **X**. The square root is evaluated in much the same way that the square root key on a pocket calculator sets a sequence of calculations in train, by the code **SQR** and the result assigned to the variable **A**. Computers do not need to store sets of tables because all the functions, and more, shown in Table 2.1, are calculated as and when required.

Table 2.1

Code	Meaning
SQR	Square root
SIN	Sine (angle in radians)
COS	Cosine (angle in radians)
TAN	Tangent (angle in radians
EXP	Raise *e* to the power
LOG	Logarithm to base *e*
INT	Largest number less than or equal to the expression

BASIC works in an *interactive* manner and this means that a programmer sitting at a PC can control the development, testing and running of a program almost instantaneously. BASIC allows the programmer to modify and edit the program being written quickly and easily. It is a language which offers a quick reaction to errors and says why it fails to understand what has been presented to it. This is particularly useful if certain things written in a program might just set a computer onto a disaster course, such as setting up an endless loop of instructions. For example, if one of the programs in Fig. 2.3 were given a set of numbers such that the program was asked to find the square root of a negative number, then this would be detected and a message sent to the programmer as the program reaches the point where the error occurs.

Fig 2.3

```
10  INPUT A,B,C
20 D = SQR(B↑2-4*A*C)/(2*A)
30 ? D
40 STOP


10  INPUT L,G
20 P=3.14159
30 T=2*P*SQR(L/G)
40 ? T
50 STOP


10  INPUT L,C
20 P=3.14159
30 F=1/(2*P*SQR(L*C))
40 ? F
50 STOP


10  INPUT X,Y
20 Z=SQR(X↑2+Y↑2)
30 ? Z
40 STOP
```

Program outline: These four programs follow the same pattern as those in Fig. 2.2 except that the expression to be evaluated contains the SQR instruction which tells the computer that the square root of whatever follows is to be evaluated.

Fig. 2.4 shows this happening with a simple program that calculates square roots of numbers. In the run shown it has been given data that forces it to try to calculate the square root of a negative number. Hence the error message. We would get a similar message if an attempt was made to divide by zero. If a key word was misspelt we would get the message **Syntax error**.

Fig 2.4

```
10  INPUT A,B
20  C=SQR(A+B)
30  ?C
40  STOP
RUN
?  3,-9
Illegal function call in 20
Ok
```

In order to help the programmer, BASIC allows us to alter lines or delete them very easily. A single line number will cause the deletion of the line with that number. The replacement of one line with another is simply done by keying in a new line with the same line number as that to be replaced. The reason why we tend to use line numbers in steps of 10 is because additional lines can be inserted in a program by using a line number between the line numbers where the insertion is to be made. For example, if a line numbered 15 was keyed in then it would automatically take its place between lines 10 and 20, assuming there were no other lines there. Most PC BASICs offer an *editor* which enables one or more characters in a line of program to be changed: a + sign to a - sign for example. An example of such program amendments is shown in Fig. 2.5.

Apart from program instructions BASIC allows us to issue *commands*. These are distinguished from program instructions by their lack of line numbers. We have already come across the **RUN** command in Fig. 2.4. There is another command which is of great use to a programmer when he wants to see the current state of his program after, for example, some changes have been made to it. The **LIST** command will cause all the program instructions to be listed out on the screen in line number order. A program can have its instructions entered in any order, last line first should you wish, but the program will always be listed and run in line number order.

Fig 2.5

```
10 INPUT X,Y
20 Z=X*Y
30 ? Z
40 STOP
RUN
? 3,4
 12
Break in 40
Ok
20 Z=X/Y
LIST
10 INPUT X,Y
20 Z=X/Y
30 ? Z
40 STOP
Ok
RUN
? 3,4
 .75
Break in 40
Ok
```

Program outline: Here we have a program that accepts two numbers, called X and Y, multiplies them together and prints this product, called Z. However, after the program has been run once, the programmer want to amend the program so that the operation of multiplication is changed to that of division. So he types in a fresh line 20, the LIST command confirms that the new line has replaced the previous line and runs the program again.

2.3 EXAMPLES

Finally here are some examples of simple BASIC programs, together with the results after they have been run. Fig. 2.6 shows a program that calculates the simple interest on the sum of money over a period of time at a particular rate of interest. Notice how we have made the program "user friendly" by using **PRINT** followed by a series of characters placed inside quotation marks. BASIC causes these lines of program to be printed exactly as they appear within the quotes, thus giving the impression that the computer is "talking" to us. The characters with quotes are called "literals" and can be any of the printing characters on the keyboard. Note also that the programs contain **REM** statements - **REM**arks which are intended to help the programmer rather than the user, who will never see them unless he lists the program. **REM** statements are included to help anyone who wishes to know exactly how the program works. In these examples the **REM** statements give little more than a program title and a very brief description. In later programs we shall see how these statements can be included in order to give "signposts" which describe what the program is doing at that particular point. **REM** statements form a useful part of the *documentation* (of which much more later) in that if a program is to be modified by someone who was not its original author then it helps in the understanding of what the author was doing at specific places in the program.

Fig 2.6

```
10 INPUT "RATE PERCENT ";R
20 INPUT "TIME IN YEARS ";T
30 INPUT "NUMBER OF POUNDS INVESTED ";P
40 I=P*T*R/100
50 PRINT P;"POUNDS INVESTED FOR ";T;"YEARS AT";R;"PERCENT PER
ANNUM"
60 PRINT "WILL GIVE YOU ";I;"POUNDS IN SIMPLE INTEREST"
70 END
RUN
RATE PERCENT ? 4.5
TIME IN YEARS ? 2
NUMBER OF POUNDS INVESTED ? 100
 100 POUNDS INVESTED FOR  2 YEARS AT   4.5 PERCENT PER ANNUM
WILL GIVE YOU  9 POUNDS IN SIMPLE INTEREST
Ok
```

Fig. 2.7 is a program which calculates the area and circumference of a circle given its radius. Note that the program has its printing controlled by semicolons (;) but in Fig. 2.8 these are replaced by commas (,) in lines 70 and 80. Note also that in line 10 a semicolon has been added at the end of the line with the result that the input request question mark is printed on the same line as the contents of line 10. This is very common practice to make a program look more conversational.

Fig 2.7

```
5 REM***PROGRAM TO CALCULATE AREA AND CIRCUMFERENCE OF
CIRCLES***
10 PRINT"TYPE RADIUS IN MM"
20 INPUT R
30 REM***CALCULATION OF AREA***
40 A=3.14159*R^2
50 REM***CALCULATION OF CIRCUMFERENCE***
60 C=2*3.14159*R
70 PRINT "AREA =";A;" SQUARE MM"
80 PRINT "CIRCUMFERENCE =";C;" MM"
90 END
RUN
TYPE RADIUS IN MM
? 300
AREA = 282743.1  SQUARE MM
CIRCUMFERENCE = 1884.945  MM
Ok
```

Fig 2.8

```
5 REM***PROGRAM TO CALCULATE AREA AND CIRCUMFERENCE OF
CIRCLES***
10 PRINT"TYPE RADIUS IN MM";
20 INPUT R
30 REM***CALCULATION OF AREA***
40 A=3.14159*R^2
50 REM***CALCULATION OF CIRCUMFERENCE***
60 C=2*3.14159*R
70 PRINT "AREA =",A," SQUARE MM"
80 PRINT "CIRCUMFERENCE =",C," MM"
90 END
RUN
TYPE IN RADIUS IN MM? 300
AREA =            282743.1        SQUARE MM
CIRCUMFERENCE =                   1884.945       MM
Ok
```

Another way of doing this is to use the line

10 INPUT "TYPE IN THE RADIUS IN MM",R

instead of the two lines 10 and 20. This technique is used in a number of programs in later chapters.

Lastly with Fig. 2.9 we have a program which illustrates one way in which the output from a program can be placed exactly where it is wanted on the screen by using the **TAB** instruction. This is particularly useful if the output is to be printed onto pre-printed stationery. **TAB** indicates exactly at what position across the page the next character is to be printed: **TAB(15)** at the 15th position, **TAB(55)** at the 55th position and so on. It is very similar to the tabbing arrangements on a normal typewriter. **TAB** will often be used in programs in subsequent chapters.

Fig 2.9

```
10 PRINT TAB(10);"HEADING"
20 PRINT TAB(8);"---------------"
30 PRINT
40 PRINT TAB(10);"JOHN";TAB(20);"JANE";TAB(30);"JIM"
50 PRINT TAB(8);"JOANNA";TAB(21);"AMY";TAB(27);"ARTHUR"
60 PRINT TAB(11);"BOB";TAB(17);"ANTHONY";TAB(25);"RODERICK"
70 END
RUN
        HEADING
        -----------------


        JOHN       JANE       JIM
        JOANNA      AMY       ARTHUR
          BOB     ANTHONY   RODERICK
Ok
```

If you wanted to print the output on your printer then the **PRINT** command is replaced by **LPRINT**. If you wish to list your program on your printer - to retain a "hard copy" - then the command is **LLIST**.

2.4 COMPILERS AND INTERPRETERS

The most common version of the BASIC language is the *interpreter* version. In this version each line of program is checked for correct syntax as the program runs. If an error is discovered then the program will stop and you can edit the offending line and often carry on from where you left off. This continual interpretation of each line of program results in slow running. If, however, you obtain a *compiler* version of the language you will be able to create a version of your program as a .EXE file. The process of *compiling* detects errors of syntax before you actually run the program. You can then edit these errors out of the original, source, program and re-compile it. The resulting, error-free, program can then be run directly from the operating system and will run far faster than any interpreter version. Most of the languages dealt with in the second half of this book are compiled ready to run by the production of a .EXE file.

DECISIONS, DECISIONS

3.1 CONDITIONAL AND UNCONDITIONAL JUMPS

In both the previous chapters it has been said that a program will proceed to execute in the order of its instructions once it has been given the **RUN** command. In BASIC programs the order of execution is determined by the *line numbers* allocated to each line of the program. The order in which the program instructions are executed can be changed by two type of instructions. One of these is the *unconditional jump* which simply says

    GOTO 400

so that the next line of program to be executed is that bearing the line number 400 irrespective of where in the program the directive is placed ("Go to gaol; go directly to gaol, do not pass Go, do not collect £200!").

On the other hand the computer can be made to take logical decisions and select one of two alternatives and this gives it a power beyond that of a simple calculating machine.

BASIC allows the programmer to write meaningful instructions which say, for example

    IF X>Y THEN GOTO 200

which will cause the instruction on line 200 to be executed only if the value of the variable **X** *exceeds* that of the variable **Y**. If the test fails then the next instruction in order is executed. This is a *conditional jump*. The test which can be made part of a conditional jump instruction can come from six possible types. These are

Greater than	>
Less than	<
Equal to	=
Not equal to	<> or #
Greater than or equal to	>=
Less than or equal to	<=

and so we can write tests of the form

    100 IF X>Y THEN GOTO 200

or

    100 IF X<Y THEN GOTO 200

or

    100 IF X=Y THEN GOTO 200

or

    100 IF X<>Y THEN GOTO 200

or

    100 IF X>=Y THEN GOTO 200

or

    100 IF X<=Y THEN GOTO 200

All six of the above tests are based on the truth, or otherwise, of the assertion that follows the word **IF**. The first of the six examples could be written in a form closer to English as

IF(the assertion that the value of X is greater than the value of Y is true) THEN the next instruction is to be found on line 200.

In general we can write any testable assertion after an **IF**; for example we can write a test that determines or not whether **I** is zero or if B^2 is greater than **4*A*C** or any relationship between variables and constants that can either be true or false. (This is an example of the *binary* nature of the workings of a computer.)

So far we have seen that if the assertion is true then a jump is made to a particular line of program. This, however, may not always be the case since most forms of BASIC allow the **IF** test to be followed by any executable BASIC statement such as **PRINT**, **STOP** or **LET** as well as **GOTO**. For example we could write

   10 IF X=Y THEN PRINT "EQUAL"

or

   10 IF X<>Y THEN LET X=Y

In fact the **IF** test can be extended to get rid of the **GOTO** statement whose use is often criticised by purist programmers. There are those who believe that the **GOTO** statement should be banned from use as it tends to lead to programs that are of spaghetti-like complexity. It is with this in mind that we can use the **IF** . . . **THEN** . . . **ELSE** . . . statement whose use will be explained in the next set of examples.

3.2 PUTTING DECISIONS TO USE

Now let us see some programs written in BASIC which illustrate the use of decisions to cause the repetition of parts of the program in order to accumulate a total. It is very tempting to write a program which looks as shown below to add up a set of numbers and produce their total and their average:

```
10  INPUT A,B,C,D,E,F,G,H,,I,J
20  T=A+B+C=D=E+F+G+H+I+J
30  PRINT "TOTAL IS";T
40  PRINT "AVERAGE IS ";T/10
```

but a moment's thought will show that it is not a very useful program since it could not be expanded - as all the examples that follow can - to accept, total and calculate the average of, say, 100 numbers. We would soon find that we had a very unwieldy program and that we had run out of letters of the alphabet!

The example in Fig. 3.1 is a program which inputs three numbers, adds them up and prints their total and average size. Notice that this is done in a loop where the number of numbers input is kept track of through a variable called

C. The running total of the numbers is held in a variable called **T**.

Fig 3.1

```
5 REM***PROGRAM TO AVERAGE A SET OF 10 NUMBERS***
10 C=0
20 T=0
30 INPUT X
40 T=T+X
50 C=C+1
60 IF C=10 THEN 80
70 GOTO 30
80 PRINT "TOTAL IS ";T
90 PRINT "AVERAGE IS ";T/10
100 END
```

Program outline: In this program the variable C and T are used to hold a count of how many numbers have been input to the program and their running total respectively. Lines 10 and 20 set these variables to be zero, since at that point no numbers have been input and their total so far is therefore zero. The numbers are input one at a time whenever line 30 is reached and at line 40 the value of T is increased by the number input at line 30. Line 50 sees C increased by one as each number is processed. Then line 60 tests the value of C to see if it has reached 10. If it has then the total and the average are printed and the program stops at line 100. If less than ten numbers have been input then line 30 is executed again to input another number. Notice that only the current value of X is retained, and as soon as line 30 is executed again a new value overwrites the previous value so we would get the following sequence. Initially, C = 0 and T = 0. At line 30 X becomes, say, 21. Then T becomes 21 and C becomes 1. The test at line 60 fails and so we go back to line 30 where X may be assigned a new value of, say, 15. T then becomes 36 and C will increase to 2. At this point the program has retained the running total of 36, the number of items input, 2 and the last value of X which was 15. The 21 has been lost for ever having been replaced by 15. And so the program continues.

Fig 3.2

```
5 REM***A BETTER VERSION OF AVERAGE PROGRAM***
10 C=0
20 T=0
25 INPUT "HOW MANY NUMBERS ";N
27 REM***CONTROLS THE NUMBER OF ITEMS INPUT***
30 INPUT X
40 T=T+X
50 C=C+1
60 IF C=N THEN 80
70 GOTO 30
80 PRINT "TOTAL IS ";T
90 PRINT "AVERAGE IS ";T/N
100 STOP
```

Program outline: This is basically the same as Fig. 3.1 except that there is a request for a number to be input at line 25 which will tell the program how many numbers it will have to total. The number will be held in the variable N instead of always being 10 as in the previous program. This means that line 60 tests C against the value of N, which could be 5 or 79 or 100 or whatever, instead of 10 and that line 90 computes the average by dividing the total by the value of N.

The program in Fig. 3.3 is an even more refined version in that the person who uses the program need have no idea of how many numbers are to be input before the program is run. To use the program in Fig. 3.2 properly the user would have to count the number of items to be processed before the program is run. Computer people are notoriously bad at arithmetic! Fig. 3.3 uses a "trigger", in this case a rogue value of X which is -1. The value -1 has no special significance, any number which does not exist in the rest of the list will do. Other common numbers used as triggers are 0, 999, 9999 and so on.

3.3 WHILE/WEND

The example shown in Fig. 3.4 shows an alternative way of writing the program should you know how many numbers are being averaged. It uses two commands that get us away from having to use the **GOTO** statement. These are **WHILE**, at the start of the loop, and **WEND** at its end. The **WHILE** statement says "While a certain condition is true repeat the instructions between here and the **WEND** statement". This produces a much "cleaner" program without

any loose ends and lends itself much more easily to
structuring.

Fig 3.3

```
5 REM***AVERAGE PROGRAM USING -1 AS A TRIGGER TO STOP
INPUT***
10 C=0
20 T=0
30 INPUT X
40 IF X=-1 THEN 80
50 T=T+X
60 C=C+1
70 GOTO 30
80 PRINT "THE TOTAL OF ";C;" NUMBERS IS ";T
90 PRINT "THE AVERAGE IS ";T/C
100 STOP
```

Fig 3.4

```
10 REM***EVEN BETTER VERSION OF AVERAGE PROGRAM***
20 TOTAL = 0
30 COUNT = 0
40 INPUT"HOW MANY NUMBERS ";N
50 WHILE COUNT<N
60 INPUT X
70 TOTAL = TOTAL+X
80 COUNT = COUNT +1
90 WEND
100 PRINT "TOTAL IS ";TOTAL
110 PRINT "AVERAGE IS ";TOTAL/N
120 STOP
```

**Program outline: This not only introduces the
WHILE/WEND constructions but it also uses names instead
of letters for the variables. The test in line 50 sees if the
value of COUNT is less than N, the number of items to be
processed. While it is the loop between lines 50 and 90 is
executed. At the point where COUNT equals N the loop is
traversed for the last time and the answers are printed.**

The next example, Fig. 3.5, uses the **WHILE/WEND**
construction in conjunction with a trigger of -1. Because
the loop between lines 50 and 90 is traversed when the
trigger value is read - remember that up to that point the
value of X is the last value read in and so the loop is
executed this last time - the count will be one too many
and the total one too small. This is adjusted in lines 100
and 110.

Fig 3.5

```
10 REM***BETTER VERSION STILL USING -1 AS A TRIGGER***
20 TOTAL = 0
30 COUNT= 0
40 X = 0
50 WHILE X<>-1
60 INPUT X
70 TOTAL = TOTAL+X
80 COUNT = COUNT+1
90 WEND
100 PRINT "TOTAL IS ";TOTAL+1
110 PRINT "AVERAGE IS ";(TOTAL+1)/(COUNT-1)
120 STOP
```

The last two examples illustrate the use that can be made of the **IF/THEN/ELSE** construction together with the useful feature of all the latest versions of BASIC that allow us to put more than one statement on a line separated by a colon (:). Fig. 3.6 uses this construction in conjunction with **GOTO** but Fig. 3.7 uses it with the **WHILE/WEND** statements to form a tight loop without any superfluous statements.

Fig 3.6

```
20 TOTAL=0:COUNT=0
30 INPUT X
40 IF X=-1 THEN PRINT "TOTAL IS ";TOTAL;"AVERAGE IS
";TOTAL/COUNT:STOP ELSE COUNT=COUNT+1:TOTAL=TOTAL+X
50 GOTO 30
60 END
```

Program outline: All the heart of this program is in line 40. Although this is quite a long line it is fairly easy to understand. If X equals -1 then the last number has already been processed in which case the total and average can be calculated and printed. Then the program stops. If this is not the case then COUNT and TOTAL are updated and line 30 is executed again.

This program uses the dreaded **GOTO** statement which is to be shunned whenever possible. Fig. 3.7 on the other hand uses the **WHILE/WEND** and **IF/THEN/ELSE** statements together.

Fig 3.7

```
10 TOTAL=0:COUNT=0
20 WHILE X<>-1
30 INPUT X
40 IF X=-1 THEN PRINT "TOTAL IS ";TOTAL;"AVERAGE IS
";TOTAL/COUNT:STOP ELSE TOTAL=TOTAL+X: COUNT=COUNT +1
50 WEND
60 STOP
```

Fig. 3.8 shows decisions put to use in a program that will perform a simple currency conversion. You should notice that it does not use **GOTO** statements unlike the version in the first two editions of this book - this goes to show how BASIC has improved over the last few years!

Fig 3.8

```
5 REM***CONVERSION PROGRAM - POUNDS TO DOLLARS OR VICE
VERSA***
10 PRINT"THIS PROGRAM WILL ALLOW YOU TO CONVERT POUNDS
STERLING"
20 PRINT"TO AMERICAN DOLLARS OR VICE VERSA"
30 INPUT "WHAT IS THE CURRENT RATE OF DOLLARS TO THE
POUND";RATE
40 PRINT"TYPE 1 FOR CONVERSION FROM POUNDS TO DOLLARS"
50 INPUT "TYPE 2 FOR CONVERSION FROM DOLLARS TO POUNDS";N
60 IF N=1 THEN INPUT "HOW MANY POUNDS TO BE CONVERTED";POUNDS
ELSE IF N=2 THEN INPUT "HOW MANY DOLLARS TO BE
CONVERTED";DOLLARS ELSE PRINT "ENTER 1 OR 2":STOP
70 IF N=1 THEN PRINT POUNDS;"POUNDS =";POUNDS*RATE;"US
DOLLARS":STOP
80 IF N=2 THEN PRINT DOLLARS;"US DOLLARS
=";DOLLARS/RATE;"POUNDS":STOP
```

Program outline: You can see how the main part of the calculation has been squeezed into lines 70 and 80 after the important test and its consequences in line 60 which sieves out wrong entries into the value for N. Notice how line 60 enables the correct questions to be asked depending on the value of N.

An example of a computer program which is non-computational is shown in the next example, Fig. 3.9, where the program sorts three numbers into ascending order. All it performs are a series of tests that result in a series of interchanges if the tests are result in a TRUE outcome. The **SWAP** function is made use of to exchange the contents of a pair of variables.

Fig 3.9

```
10 INPUT A,B,C
20 IF A>B THEN SWAP A,B
30 IF B>C THEN SWAP B,C
40 IF A>B THEN SWAP A,B
50 PRINT A,B,C
```

Program outline: If you find this program confusing try to follow it out by writing numbers on three pieces of paper and performing the swaps whenever needed. All you have to do is examine the first pair of numbers: if they are not in order, swap them over. Then examine the next pair of numbers and do the same thing. Then examine the first pair again and swap if necessary. The best test is to see if it works with three numbers in descending order:

9   8   7

look at first two - swap

8   9   7

now the second two - swap

8   7   9

now the first two again - swap

7   8   9

and they are now in ascending order.

3.4 FOR/NEXT loops

In some of the preceding examples a loop of instructions has been traversed by setting up a starting value of a counting variable, going through a loop, incrementing the variable and then testing to see how many times the loop has been executed. Fig. 3.2 was a good example of this. All high-level languages allow us to define loops by means of special instructions thus reducing the amount of code the programmer has to write; the **WHILE/WEND** instructions are a case in point. In BASIC this can be done effectively by means of the **FOR . . . NEXT . . .** loop when other methods cannot be used. At the start of the loop we could, for example, write

FOR I = 1 TO 10 STEP 1

and at the end of the loop write

NEXT I

The first of this pair of instructions states that the counting variable is to be called **I** and it is initially to be set to have a value of **1**. **I** is to be increased in steps of **1** until it has reached **10**. When **I** has reached the value of **10** the loop is no longer executed and the instruction immediately following the **NEXT I** line is to be executed. The loop of instructions is therefore bracketed by the **FOR** . . . and the **NEXT** . . . so that

```
10 FOR I = 1 TO 10 STEP 1
20 PRINT I
30 NEXT I
```

will result in the numbers 1 to 10 being displayed. In the same way

```
10 FOR I = 10 TO 1 STEP -1
20 PRINT I
30 NEXT I
```

will result in the numbers 10 down to 1 being displayed. If the step size is 1 then it can be omitted so that

```
FOR I = 1 TO 10
```

implies a step size of 1.

The foregoing may be trivial examples, but look at Fig. 3.10 where ten numbers are read in prior to their total and average being displayed. The program shown in Fig. 3.11 shows the same process taking place but for a number of inputs governed by the number allocated to **N** in line 10. Both these programs are similar to those in Figs 3.1 and 3.2.

Fig 3.10

```
1 REM***ANOTHER AVERAGING PROGRAM USING 'FOR - NEXT' LOOP FOR
INPUT***
5 T = 0
10 FOR I = 1 TO 10 STEP 1
20 INPUT X
30 T = T + X
40 NEXT I
```

```
50 A = T/10
60 ? T,A
70 END
```

Program outline: here is yet another version of the program which averages a set of numbers. It uses the BASIC facility of defining a loop of instructions which are bracketed by the statements in lines 10 and 40. Line 10 says that the value of the variable called I must go from 1 to 10 in steps of 1 and line 40 says that it is at this point that the value of I is incremented. This means that the loop contained within lines 20 and 30 will be repeated 10 times. After the loop has been executed 10 times line 50 will be executed followed by the rest of the program.

Fig 3.11

```
1 REM***THE VALUE OF N CONTROLS THE NUMBER OF TIMES THE LOOP
IS EXECUTED***
5 T = 0
10 INPUT N
20 FOR I = 1 TO N STEP 1
30 INPUT X
40 T = T + X
50 NEXT I
60 A = T/N
70 ? T,A
80 END
```

Program outline: This is basically the same as the program in Fig. 3.10 except that the number of times the loop is traversed is held in the variable N which is input at line 10.

The program that is shown in Fig. 3.12 uses a **FOR . . . NEXT . . .** loop to control the display of the values of the expression

$$4x^2 + 3x - 2$$

over a range of values of **X**.

Fig 3.12

```
5 REM***EXAMPLE OF A LOOP WITH START, FINISH AND INCREMENT
DETERMINED AT RUN TIME***
10 INPUT F,L,S
20 FOR X = F TO L STEP S
30 Y=4*X^2+3*X-2
40 ? Y
```

```
50 NEXT X
60 END
```

Program outline: The program would be very useful if a table of values of a certain expression were required. At line 10 three numbers are input which will define the starting value, F, of the variable called X, the largest value, L, for X and the size of the step, S, by which F is to be incremented from F to L. In other words, if F was made 1, L made 6 and S was 0.5 then the values of Y would be calculated for values of X which would be in turn

1, 1.5, 2, 2.5, 3 . . . . . . 5, 5.5, 6

Once X has reached 6 the last calculation and display are made and the program stops.

STORING DATA IN MEMORY

4.1 STORING LISTS

We have already seen that the variable names in BASIC act as *symbolic addresses* for storage in RAM. However, it is also possible to store lists of numbers in memory by using what is called in BASIC a **DIM** statement. **DIM** stands for **DIM**ension and reserves space in RAM for a set of variables which all have a common family name. For example

     10 DIM K(100)

will cause a set of memory locations to be set aside for a list whose members are known individually as **K(1)**, **K(2)**, **K(3)**, up to **K(100)**. It is rather like reserving a set of rooms in an hotel for a large party.

Fig. 4.1 shows a simple program in BASIC to read a set of numbers into a list and then display them on the screen. The object of the program is to place a series of numbers into a set of related addresses ready for immediate access while the program is running. But beware - if another program is then entered and run then the set of numbers previously put into the list *cannot be retrieved*. Any other program cannot access variables stored in RAM by another program unless special techniques are used. The easiest way to do such a thing is to store the data away on disk, not in RAM. The techniques used for this will be dealt with in Chapter 5.

Another example of the simple use to which the storage of data in a list is put is in the program featured in Fig. 4.2. In this a randomly organised set of numbers is read into a list and then the list is scanned in order to find the smallest number in the list. (Note that the method used for triggering off the end of the input list is also used in the program shown in Fig. 3.3.) The program scans through the list from the start comparing each number with the smallest number found so far as it goes. This routine has to be started off and this is achieved by first of all allocating the very first number in the list to be the smallest number, which it is at that point. Then the second number is compared with the smallest and if it is smaller then this number takes over the role of the current smallest. Then the third number in the list is compared with the current smallest and so on until the end of the list is reached. At that point the smallest number is printed out. The repetition of the "test - replace the smallest so far by the number it is tested against if this is now smaller - go to the next number in the list" is just the kind of repetitive operation a computer can do, never get tired of and perform faster than we can.

Fig 4.1

```
5 REM***USING A LIST OF NUMBERS IN MEMORY***
10 DIM L(50)
20 INPUT N
30 FOR I = 1 TO N
35 REM***ALLOCATES NUMBERS TO THE LIST - ONE AT A TIME***
40 INPUT L(I)
50 NEXT I
60 FOR I = 1 TO N
65 REM***DISPLAYS LIST L STORED IN MEMORY - ONE AT A TIME***
70 PRINT L(I)
80 NEXT I
90 END
```

Program outline: This program serves no really useful purpose except to show how we can set up lists of numbers in RAM. What we can do with these lists is a matter for explanation in other programs which will follow later. A list of numbers is stored in memory (RAM). Any data stored in this type of memory can be read far faster than if it was on a backing store such as disks or tape. RAM has no moving parts and is all-electronic whereas backing store will always, until new technology provides something faster, contain much slower mechanical devices. However, there is a disadvantage to storing data in RAM in that it has to share the memory with the program which is used to manipulate the data and as soon as another program is loaded into RAM, or the computer is switched off, everything in memory is lost.

The first line of the program prepares the ground for a list called L which is to have 50 numbers stored in it. They will be known as L(1), L(2), L(3), . . . , L(50). At line 20 the variable N is given a value which determines how much of the list we actually wish to use. N can have any value so long as it does not exceed 50 - see below for the effect of N exceeding 50. Once N has been given a value then the number of times the first of the two loops is to be executed is established. By this the required number of items are placed in the list. If N is 20 then only 20 numbers will be accepted by the program. The first number input will be assigned the name of L(1), the second L(2) and so on, so that the Nth number is placed in L(N). By this time the numbers in the list have been placed in RAM and can be accessed for whatever processing the program requires. In our preliminary example all we are going to do is simply copy the list from RAM onto the screen. The second loop starts off a counter, called I back to 1 and then proceeds to display all the list in turn, starting at L(1) and finishing with L(N), on the screen.

If, in line 20, N had been given a value of, say, 55 then the program would have gone well and accepted the first 50 numbers input putting them into the list L. However, when I reached the value of 51, which is one more than the DIMensioning statement in the first line of the program has allowed for, an error message would be displayed saying

SUBSCRIPT OUT OF RANGE IN 40

which tells us that we are trying to use an item in a list with a subscript (the number in brackets) which has not been allowed for, in this case the 51st. Only by reDIMensioning the list with a larger number, say DIM L(55), and starting again from the beginning will the problem go away.

4.2 SORTING LISTS INTO ORDER

The example in Fig. 4.2 may appear at first to be trivial but in fact it forms the basis of a very useful program which is used to sort numbers into ascending order, another time-consuming and boring task when done by hand. The technique is to scan the unsorted list to find the smallest number. This number is placed at the head of a new list and the original list scanned again to find the next smallest number. This is then placed in the second position in the new list, and the next smallest number found, placed in the new list and so on. The problem that immediately arises is once the smallest number in the list has been found, how do we find the next smallest? One way of doing this is if, once the smallest number has been and copied into the new list, its place is taken by a large number, say 99999 as in our example. The routine for finding the smallest in the list is then used again. Once the next smallest is found

Fig 4.2

```
5 REM***PROGRAM TO LOCATE THE SMALLEST NUMBER IN A LIST***
10 DIM L(50)
15 I=1
20 INPUT L(I)
30 IF L(I)=-1 THEN 100
40 I=I+1
50 GOTO 20
100 N=I-1
101 I=1
105 S=L(I)
110 I=I+1
120 IF I>N THEN 200
125 REM***CURRENT SMALLEST FOUND AND ASSIGNED TO S***
130 IF S>L(I) THEN S=L(I)
140 GOTO 110
200 PRINT S
210 END
```

Program outline: The maximum size of the list L is DIMensioned in line 10 and then a set of numbers are read into that list, counted in by the variable I. The list is terminated by a -1 trigger. Since the last item in the list is to be ignored because it is -1 the actual length of the list is called N which is equal to I - 1, line 100. The list is now scanned from the first, where I = 1, to the last, where I = N, to establish which is the smallest number in the list, S. In line 130 the current smallest, S, is tested against each element of the list in turn, L(I), and if S exceeds L(I) then S assumes the value of that element. That all sounds fine but remember that S has to have some initial value and that is why we have line 105 which sets the first value of S to the value of L(1). After all, if we are looking at the members of the list one at a time in order then while we are looking at the first in the list it is the smallest so far. Notice that the loop never takes the program back to line 105 again; the loop takes us from line 140 to line 110 and we only drop out of the loop by succeeding in the test on line 120 when we have reached the end of the list and display the value of S. Then the program stops.

then it too can be replaced by 99999 and the routine continues until such time as the original list contains nothing but 99999s. At that point the new list must contain all the numbers in ascending order. The program is shown in Fig. 4.3.

Fig 4.3

```
5 REM***SORTING BY SELECTION OF THE CURRENT SMALLEST IN A
LIST***
10 DIM A(100),B(100)
15 REM**INPUT PHASE**
20 I=1
30 INPUT A(I)
40 IF A(I)=-1 THEN 70
50 I=I+1
60 GOTO 30
70 N=I-1
74 REM**END OF INPUT PHASE**
75 L=1
80 S=A(1)
81 J=1
85 K=0
90 FOR I=1 TO N
100 IF S>A(I) THEN 200
110 IF A(I)=99999! THEN K=K+1
120 NEXT I
140 GOTO 250
200 S=A(I)
210 J=I
220 GOTO 120
250 B(L)=S
255 L=L+1
256 REM***REPLACEMENT OF CURRENT SMALLEST BY 99999***
260 A(J)=99999!
265 IF K=N-1 THEN 300
270 GOTO 80
300 B(L)=S
304 REM***DISPLAYING THE SORTED LIST***
305 FOR I=1 TO N
310 PRINT B(I);
320 NEXT I
330 END
```

Program outline: This program uses two lists, A and B, which can contain up to 100 numbers each. First of all the unsorted list is read into list A, lines 20 to 70, using the trigger to again to indicate the end of the list. The variable L is set to 1 in line 75 and keeps track of how many of the numbers have been placed in list B. Line 80 sets the first value of S, the smallest number, to be the first number in list A. The variable J, initially at 1, tells us which number in list A contains the current smallest. This is because we have been right through the list and discovered the smallest number it contains and we need to know where it is so that we can replace it with 99999. The variable K keeps count of the number of 99999s placed in list A. Once list A has been scanned and the current smallest number has been found it is placed in the next available place in list B, its place in list A is filled with 99999 and the list is scanned again for the next smallest. When there is only one number in list A, and it is not 99999 (tested in line 265) then that number is placed into list B and the sorted list displayed; lines 305 to 320. Then the program stops.

If the program in Fig. 4.3 is used to sort very long lists of numbers it soon becomes slow and inefficient. This is because the whole list is continually scanned from end to end each time and there will be more and more unnecessary tests. The version shown in Fig. 4.4 is a more elegant approach to the problem. In this case the unsorted list becomes shorter and shorter as the current smallest number is pulled out of the list. Once the position of the smallest number has been established, all those members of the list that follow it are squeezed up by one place. The sorting process then becomes faster and faster as the list becomes shorter and shorter. When the list only contains one number the sort is complete. The examples shown in this section, that is in Figs 4.2 to 4.4, all use **GOTO** statements which make the tracing of the program quite complex. It has already been said that these statements should be avoided whenever possible and so the example in Fig. 4.5 is an amended version of Fig. 4.4 using **WHILE/WEND** and a lengthy **IF ... THEN ...** statement. You should see that it produces a shorter and neater program and you would find it very good practice to amend the other programs in this section in the same way.

Fig. 4.6 shows another program for sorting numbers, but this time the list is scanned from start to finish and pairs of numbers which are such that the first is greater than the second are switched round. This method is known as a *bubble* sort since the numbers are constantly moving along the list and the larger numbers rise towards the top of the list, like the bubbles in a fizzy drink. When the list has been scanned without any interchange of adjacent numbers taking place the list known to be sorted and the program stops. The program can sense that no interchange has been made by the use of a variable called a *flag* which is set to 1 whenever an interchange routine has been performed. At the start of the scan the value of the flag is set to zero and at the end of the scan the flag is tested to see it has changed in value. If it has not then no changes have been made to the list and hence this implies that the sorting process is complete. Again, the method is not very efficient if long lists of numbers are being sorted.

Fig. 4.6 shows a more efficient method called a *shell* sort. It is a version of the bubble sort. It is always a good idea to test out a program such as this with dummy data and trace its progress through the program with pencil and paper. This is often called a *dry run* and can be very revealing.

Fig 4.4

```
5 REM***A FASTER VERSION OF SELECTION SORT***
10 DIM A(100),B(100)
20 I=1
30 INPUT A(I)
40 IF A(I)=-1 THEN 70
50 I=I+1
60 GOTO 30
70 N=I-1
75 L=1
80 S=A(1)
85 J=1
90 FOR I=1 TO N
100 IF S>A(I) THEN 200
110 NEXT I
120 N=N-1
130 IF N=0 THEN 400
140 GOTO 300
200 S=A(I)
210 J=I
220 GOTO 110
300 B(L)=A(J)
310 L=L+1
315 REM***THIS SECTION MOVES THE REST OF THE LIST UP ONE
PLACE***
320 FOR K=J TO N
330 A(K)=A(K+1)
340 NEXT K
350 GOTO 80
395 REM***DISPLAY SORTED LIST***
400 B(L)=A(1)
401 FOR J=1 TO L
410 PRINT B(J);
420 NEXT J
430 STOP
```

Program outline: This is very similar to the program in Fig. 4.3 except that instead of replacing the elements of list A by a rogue value of 99999 as the current smallest is discovered the list is made to shrink so that if at any point, say, the fifth element of the list is found to be the smallest then after it has been copied into the sorted list, list B, all the rest of the list from A(6) onward is shifted up one place. This is done in lines 320 to 340. The effect of this is to shorten the list by one item each time it is scanned, thus making the scanning faster and faster as there become less and less elements to scan. Notice that the value of N is reduced by one in line 120 each time the list is scanned until N becomes zero in line 130. At this point the program is directed to line 400 when the last remaining number in list A is placed at the end of list B which is then displayed. Then the program ends.

Fig 4.5

```
5 REM***A FASTER VERSION OF SELECTION SORT***
10 DIM A(100),B(100)
20 I=1
30 WHILE X<>-1
40 INPUT X
45 A(I)=X
50 I=I+1
60 WEND
70 N=I-2
75 L=1
79 WHILE N<>0
80 S=A(1)
85 J=1
90 FOR I=1 TO N
100 IF S>A(I) THEN S=A(I):J=I
120 N=N-1
130 IF N=0 THEN B(L)=A(1):FOR J=1 TO L: PRINT B(J);:NEXT
J:STOP
300 B(L)=A(J)
310 L=L+1
315 REM***THIS SECTION MOVES THE REST OF THE LIST UP ONE
PLACE***
320 FOR K=J TO N
330 A(K)=A(K+1)
340 NEXT K
350 WEND
```

Fig 4.6

```
5 REM***SORTING USING THE BUBBLE SORT***
10 DIM L(100)
20 I=1
30 WHILE X<>-1
40 INPUT X
45 L(I)=X
50 I=I+1
60 WEND
70 N=I-2
80 F=1
81 WHILE F=1
82 F=0
85 REM**START SCANNING THE LIST**
90 FOR I = 1 TO N-1
95 REM**COMPARE ADJACENT ITEMS IN THE LIST**
100 IF L(I)>L(I+1) THEN SWAP L(I),L(I+1):F=1
110 NEXT I
115 REM**TEST TO SEE IF ANY EXCHANGES HAVE BEEN MADE**
120 IF F=0 THEN FOR I=1 TO N:PRINT L(I);:NEXT I:STOP ELSE F=1
130 WEND
```

Program outline: The method of placing unsorted numbers into the list L is the same as in the previous programs. However, once the list has been established we set a flag called F to zero. Then the list is scanned from start to finish testing pairs of adjacent numbers. Should the first be greater than the second they are swapped over and the flag F is set to have a value of 1. After the whole list has been scanned the state of the flag is tested, line 120. Should this be zero then the whole list has been scanned without any exchanges being made and so the list has been sorted and it is printed in order.

Fig 4.7

```
5 REM***SORTING USING THE SHELL SORT***
10 DIM A(100)
20 I=1
30 WHILE X<>-1
40 INPUT X
50 A(I)=X
60 I=I+1
70 WEND
80 N=I-2
120 M=N
130 WHILE M>0
140 M=INT(M/2)
160 IF M<=0 THEN PRINT "Sorted List":FOR I=1 TO N:PRINT
A(I);:NEXT I:STOP
180 K=N-M
200 J=1
```

```
210 WHILE J<=K
220 I=J
230 WHILE I>0
240 R=I+M
260 IF A(I)>A(R) THEN SWAP A(R),A(I):I=I-M:WEND
380 J=J+1
400 WEND
420 WEND
```

Program outline: This shell sort program starts off by reading in the list of unsorted numbers into list A. Then a scanning takes place, but only of corresponding elements in two halves of the list. Should the order of size of the numbers compared be such that the first exceeds the second they are exchanged, line 260. Then the list is subdivided into four parts and comparable elements from the four parts are tested. This testing, moving and subdivision continues until the number of subdivisions of the list is equal to the number of elements in the list. At this point the list is sorted and can be printed out, line 160. This method of sorting is at least three times faster than the bubble sort shown in Fig. 4.6, but the principle is complex and its details are beyond the scope of this book. You should notice the use of WHILE/WEND and the way they pair up to bracket the loop.

4.3 TABLES

An extension of the concept of a list can be made by adding a second dimension so that the contents of a *table* can be stored in RAM. A table, or *array*, of numbers, say with three rows and four columns, is stored row by row so that an array called **P** with three rows and four columns would represent a table

P(1,1)	**P(1,2)**	**P(1,3)**	**P(1,4)**
P(2,1)	**P(2,2)**	**P(2,3)**	**P(2,4)**
P(3,1)	**P(3,2)**	**P(3,3)**	**P(3,4)**

where the order of the numbers in the brackets refers to the Row followed by the Column number - **P(R,C)**.

A good example of the use of an array is in a program which creates a league table for, say, a football team. The program in Fig. 4.8 demonstrates this. Note that all that is required is a set of four numbers in order: these represent the home team number, the away team number, and the goals scored by each. For example, if home team number 4 was at home to team number 2 and the scores were 3 for the home team and 1 for the away team then the four numbers 4,2,3,1 would be input to the program. This gives sufficient information to the program for the appropriate rows and columns of the league table to be amended. The contents of the first column give the number of matches played by each team, so that the element 3,1 will contain the number of games played by team number 3. The fifth column contains the number of goals scored by the teams so that element 6,5 will contain the number of goals scored by team number 6.

Fig 4.8

```
10 DIM R(10,7)
20 INPUT T1,T2,G1,G2
30 IF T1=-1 THEN 290
40 R(T1,1)=R(T1,1)+1
50 R(T2,1)=R(T2,1)+1
60 IF G1=G2 THEN 150
70 IF G1>G2 THEN 220
80 R(T1,3)=R(T1,3)+1
90 R(T1,5)=R(T1,5)+G1
100 R(T1,6)=R(T1,6)+G2
110 R(T2,2)=R(T2,2)+1
120 R(T2,6)=R(T2,6)+G1
130 R(T2,5)=R(T2,5)+G2
140 GOTO 20
150 R(T1,4)=R(T1,4)+1
160 R(T2,4)=R(T2,4)+1
170 R(T2,5)=R(T2,5)+G2
180 R(T2,6)=R(T2,6)+G1
190 R(T1,5)=R(T1,5)+G1
200 R(T1,6)=R(T1,6)+G2
210 GOTO 20
220 R(T1,2)=R(T1,2)+1
230 R(T2,6)=R(T2,6)+G1
240 R(T2,5)=R(T2,5)+G2
250 R(T2,3)=R(T2,3)+1
260 R(T1,5)=R(T1,5)+G1
270 R(T1,6)=R(T1,6)+G2
290 PRINT"TEAM  P   W   L   D   FOR   AGT   PTS"
300 PRINT"======================================="
310 FOR I=1 TO 10
320 PRINT I;
330 PRINT SPC(2);R(I,1);SPC(2);R(I,2);
340 PRINT SPC(2);R(I,3);SPC(2);R(I,4);
350 PRINT SPC(2);R(I,5);SPC(2);R(I,6);
360 PRINT SPC(2);R(I,7)
370 NEXT I
```

4.4 STRINGS

The final topic in this chapter refers to the ability of BASIC to handle *strings* of characters, denoted in BASIC by the $ sign after the variable name. A string variable is written, for example, as F$, N1$, T2$ and so on. The contents of a string variable are distinguished from other variables in that they are enclosed in quotation marks, just as *literals* are in PRINT statements. In fact the PRINT statement

300 PRINT "THIS IS THE END"

is instructing the computer to display the string of characters enclosed in the quotes. We can write statements such as

10 A$ = "DEMONSTRATION"

or

10 A$ = "A"

but we must not write

10 A$ = A

since BASIC will be fooled into thinking that we are trying to assign the value of a numeric variable, A, to a string variable, A$. This is not allowed and will result in the

Type mismatch

error message appearing on the screen. This is because characters and numbers are stored in *totally different ways* and cannot possibly be equivalent. For example if we write

10 A$ = "MACMILLAN"

then the nine characters which go to make up the word are stored in successive bytes in RAM, one byte per character. The only operation that can be performed on a string, apart from displaying it on the screen, is that of *concatenation*. The program in Fig. 4.9 illustrates this.

Fig 4.9

```
10 INPUT A$
20 INPUT B$
30 C$=A$+B$
40 PRINT C$
50 C$=A$+" "+B$
60 PRINT C$
70 END
RUN
? UNITED
? STATES
UNITEDSTATES
UNITED STATES
```

What happens in the program in Fig. 4.9 is that when two strings are concatenated one is appended onto the end of the other. Because a space is a character the second concatenation has a space included in order to improve the legibility.

Names can be sorted into alphabetical order in just the same way as numbers. A set of names put in a list can be sorted using an almost identical program to that for sorting numbers, as Fig. 4.10 shows.

Fig 4.10

```
5 REM***SORTING NAMES INTO ALPHABETICAL ORDER***
10 DIM L$(100)
20 I=1
30 WHILE X$<>"ZZZZ"
40 INPUT X$
45 L$(I)=X$
50 I=I+1
60 WEND
70 N=I-2
80 F=1
81 WHILE F=1
82 F=0
85 REM**START SCANNING THE LIST**
90 FOR I = 1 TO N-1
95 REM**COMPARE ADJACENT ITEMS IN THE LIST**
100 IF L$(I)>L$(I+1) THEN SWAP L$(I),L$(I+1):F=1
110 NEXT I
115 REM**TEST TO SEE IF ANY EXCHANGES HAVE BEEN MADE**
120 IF F=0 THEN FOR I=1 TO N:PRINT L$(I)+" ";:NEXT I:STOP
ELSE F=1
130 WEND
```

Program outline: This uses the same bubble sort technique as in the program in Fig. 4.6. The only difference is that the list of names is a list of strings and hence is called L$ rather than L.

Strings can be divided up into *substrings* by use of the commands **LEFT$**, **RIGHT$** and **MID$**. If a string named **NAME$** contains the characters "**MACMILLAN**" then we can write, for example:

    LEFT$(NAME$,4)   **MACM**
    RIGHT$(NAME$,5)   **ILLAN**
    MID$(NAME$,5,1)   **I**

where the first extracts the leftmost four characters, the second extracts the 5 rightmost characters and the third extracts the single character from the string beginning at the fifth character. A program to show this is illustrated in Fig. 4.11.

Fig 4.11

```
10 INPUT S$
20 PRINT S$;" CONTAINS ";LEN(S$);" CHARACTERS"
30 INPUT A
40 PRINT LEFT$(S$,A); " ARE THE ";A;" LEFTMOST CHARACTERS"
50 PRINT RIGHT$(S$,A);" ARE THE ";A;" RIGHTMOST CHARACTERS"
```

This program also uses the **LEN** function that provides us with the number of characters - the **LEN**gth - of a string.
   The last example in this chapter shows one use of string functions to count the number of vowels in a word.

Fig 4.12

```
10 V$="AEIOU"
20 INPUT "TYPE IN A WORD";W$
30 FOR I=1 TO LEN(W$)
40 FOR J=1 TO 5
50 IF MID$(W$,I,1)=MID$(V$,J,1) THEN V=V+1
60 NEXT J
70 NEXT I
80 PRINT W$;" CONTAINS";V;" VOWELS"
90 STOP
```

Program outline: This program uses two loops, the first to scan the word input character by character and the second to match each letter in turn with the five vowels stored in the string V$. When a match is found the counter V is incremented and when the end of the word is reached this number is displayed.

THE ELECTRONIC
FILING CABINET

5.1 INTRODUCTION

Much of the power of a computer system comes from its
ability to store and retrieve large quantities of data. The
dusty books and ledgers of the old-fashioned office are
now outmoded since all the information they contain can
now be stored on magnetic tape or magnetic disks taking
up a very small amount of space. Of course, the stored data
has to be converted into special codes which are technically
necessary for the transcription onto a magnetic medium.
Luckily, the computer software will handle this encoding
and all the programmer has to do is to decide what data is
to be placed on what computer file. This is similar to the
storage of music and speech on a gramophone record or
recording tape, for in that case we do not need to be more
than vaguely aware of the technology of the stereo disk,
cassette tape or compact disk in order to use them. So long
as we appreciate the advantages and disadvantages of the
various types of storage media, then that is enough. The
storage of computer data has many parallels with audio
technology. Both disks and tape are used and each has
specific and very good reasons for being used the way it is.
In fact, some of the hardware used in both computers and
audio is identical since microcomputers can use audio tapes
for storing both files of data and programs. More recently
the use of *CD-ROM*s (Compact Disk Read Only Memories)
is coming along for very high density storage of data. For
example, every post code in the United Kingdom is
available on one 5 inch Compact Disk. So far, however,
CD-ROMs are only available as WORMs (Write Once Read
Many times). The disks used on computers are not the same
as vinyl gramophone disks but more like, if such a thing
were possible, a flat piece of recording tape. Computer

were possible, a flat piece of recording tape. Computer disks are reusable, but gramophone records are not, except as flower pots! The advantage of using disks for the storage of data is that any piece of data can easily and quickly be retrieved by setting the *reading head* over the location of that data on the disk. Reading data stored on tape is very different since reading can take place only in sequence starting at the beginning of the tape. This is why a disk is essentially a *random access* device but a tape is a *serial access* device. Each system has its own merits. A tape has to be wound past the reading head until the required piece of data, or piece of music, is found. This can take a very significant time especially if what is required is near the end of the tape. The reading of the required data from a disk, however, is far faster than from a tape since all that is required is for the correct track on the disk to be selected and the only time lag is in waiting for the correct part of the track to appear under the head.

Most computers need one or more magnetic disks in order to work efficiently. The smallest micro-computer will take a floppy disk whose diameter is 3 inch, $3\frac{1}{2}$ inches or $5\frac{1}{4}$ inches and these can hold anything from 360,000 bytes of data up to 1.44 million bytes. Many micro-computers these days are equipped with a *hard disk* as well as one or more floppy disks and these can store anything from 10 million bytes of data upwards. A large *mainframe* computer will have a number of disk drives each with a pack of disks storing hundreds of millions of bytes each. Magnetic tape is not so commonly used in the day-to-day running of many computers but will often be used for the backing up of files for long term security storage.

5.2 SERIAL FILES

Most computer systems actually hold both serial files and direct access files on disk. Serial files are easier for the beginner to deal with and understand. Special techniques have to be used when handling direct access files in practice, so only simple applications will be dealt with in this book.

Disk or tape storage can be used to retain files of program instructions over long periods and the computer software is used for this purpose. If one writes a program which is to be used more than once, then after it has been tested and found error-free it can be saved for future use by a single command such as

SAVE "PROGNAME"

where the name of the program is displayed, often within quotation marks, as shown above. The name must be *unique to that program*.

The **SAVE** command enables a copy of the program currently in RAM to be transferred to disk. The name of the program is automatically entered into a directory of names on that disk. This enables the software to keep track of the program files stored on that disk so that they can be located and retrieved whenever they are required.

To retrieve a program from disk the command

LOAD "PROGNAME"

is used. The software examines the disk directory to establish that a file of that name actually does exist. Having done that the location of the file on the disk is discovered and a copy of the program file is loaded into RAM. The program is now in memory and ready to run just as if it had been laboriously typed in at the keyboard (see Fig. 5.1).

Fig 5.1

```
new
Ok
10 input a,b,c
20 m=(a+b+c)/3
30 ? "The average of the three numbers is ";m
40 end
save"average"
Ok
list
10 INPUT A,B,C
20 M=(A+B+C)/3
30 ? "The average of the three numbers is ";M
40 END
Ok
new
list
Ok
load"average"
Ok
run
? 3,7,8
The average of the three numbers is  6
Ok
```

Program outline: The first line in Fig. 5.1 is the command **NEW** typed in by the programmer. This clears any lines of program from RAM. Then the program is typed in line by line, a simple program to calculate the average of three numbers. It does not matter whether you type it in capital letters or not. The command SAVE"AVERAGE" will cause a copy of the program in memory to be saved onto disk. At this point there exist two versions of the program: one in memory and one on disk. The one in memory is ready for immediate execution and the one on disk is stored under the name "AVERAGE". As proof that the copy does exist in memory the command LIST causes the list of program instructions to be displayed on the screen. Notice that the letters Ok are displayed whenever the computer has had its turn. The programmer types NEW which clears all the program instructions out of RAM. This is demonstrated by the effect of the LIST command now. All that happens is that Ok appears showing that there are no program instructions in RAM to be carried out. The programmer keys in LOAD "AVERAGE", which causes the instructions stored under that name on disk to be copied into RAM. The original set of instructions have now be restored to RAM from disk and the command RUN causes them to be executed and the program asks for the three numbers, computes their average and prints the answer according to the instructions in the program.

You may notice that the words *program file* were used just before Fig. 5.1. This is because a program is simply a collection of characters which have no life of their own until they are presented to BASIC by the **RUN** command. (See Fig. 5.1 for an example of a program being **SAVE**d, **LOAD**ed and **RUN**.) Remember, a program in memory is there only while the computer is switched on and until you type **NEW** or **LOAD** another program. A program on disk is there permanently until someone deliberately destroys it with a **DELETE** or **KILL** command. Fig. 5.2 shows a copy of a disk directory, under the MS-DOS operating system, where the extension .BAS indicates that a file is a BASIC program file, .DAT indicates a data file and .TXT text file.

When dealing with data files, as opposed to program files, there are three operations which must be mastered:

(1)   Putting data into a file for permanent storage.
(2)   Copying the data stored in a file to some display device such as a printer or a video screen.
(3)   Amending the data stored in a data file.

Fig 5.2

```
DIR
  Volume in drive A is BASIC
  Directory of    A:\

PROG1     BAS 24990   20-01-89      1.59a
TOP       TXT   408   20-01-89      2:10a
FIG411    BAS 23829   20-01-89      1:40p
PROG2     DAT 35401   20-01-89     12:23a
  .
  .
  .
  .
  11 File(s)           123904 bytes free
```

The directory listing in Fig. 5.2 gives the number of bytes of disk storage taken up by each file and the date and time when it was saved.

A good example of putting these operations to good use would be the setting up, maintenance and printing of a mailing list of names and addresses stored on disk. A program has to be written which will accept the names and addresses from a keyboard, and place them in some sort of order onto a disk file. Next there must be a program which will read the data from the file and print them onto sticky labels ready to be affixed to envelopes. The format of the output is shown in Fig. 5.3.

Fig 5.3

Mr J Smith
12 The Park
Cheltenham
Gloucs
GL3 5TR

Mr John Watson
Peabody Buildings
Streatham
London
SW10 5RD

Mr D Knight
Waverley Court
Upper Norwood
London
NE4 7YT

Mrs J Knight
34 Park Road
Midhurst
Hants
FA3 7TR

Mr D Swift
3 Fleet Road
Oldbury
Lancs
OH4 6TW

Miss J Harrow
Laurels, Park St
Harhill
Suffolk
CL4 6QA

A moment's thought will show that this is not a trivial task. Printers print one line only across a page at a time, so that three names and addresses have to be printed in the width of the page in the following manner:

name1	name2	name3
street1	street2	street3
town1	town2	town3
county1	county2	county3
postcode1	postcode2	postcode3

Finally, a program is needed which will maintain the name and address file and keep it up to date. This means that it must be capable of deleting out-of-date entries and modifying addresses when people remain on file and move house or when incorrect addresses are on the file.

5.3 USE OF FILES IN PROGRAMS

The first type of program - writing data to a file - requires that the programmer first of all asks for space to be made ready on the disk to receive the data. This is the operation of **OPEN**ing a file, which must bear a *unique* name, entering its name in the disk directory and making it ready for data to be written to it. Such a program statement might be

```
OPEN "O",1,"Names"
```

where the "O" denotes that the file is an **O**utput file, that is, one that is to be written to. The number is an identification number, sometimes called a "channel" or a "stream". Its use is seen when you look at the programs in Figs 5.4 and 5.5. The name of the file is enclosed in quotation marks at the end of the line. When data is transferred to the file you can use

```
WRITE#1,variable name
```

where the number after the # (hash) sign is the channel or stream number. This is because you may want to write to more than one file in a program and you need some means of identifying the different files. Fig. 5.4 shows a program to input a series of names and addresses into a serial file called **Names**.

Fig. 5.4

```
10 OPEN "O",1,"Names"
22 WHILE A$<>"ZZZ"
23 INPUT "Surname"; A$
25 IF A$="ZZZ" THEN STOP
30 INPUT "Title & Initials";B$
```

```
40 INPUT "Street";C$
50 INPUT "Town";D$
60 INPUT "County";E$
70 INPUT "Post code";F$
80 WRITE#1,A$,B$,C$,D$,E$,F$
90 WEND
```

Program outline: The file is defined and opened for business in line 10. The loop is traversed until the variable called A$ is given a value of ZZZ at which point the program stops. Each of the variables are written onto the file serially so that until the trigger tells the program to stop, and in doing so will close the file down, it loops round and writes a series of records to the file. Only you, the programmer, knows that they represent in turn the surname, initials and address lines for a series of people.

To read the data back and display it on the screen another program has to be written that will read each record serially from the beginning of the file and display it on the screen in a specified format. The first instruction that is needed is an instruction to open the file ready for reading

OPEN "I",1,"Names"

which states that a file called **Names**, on channel 1, is to be opened for Input. The effect is that the data coming from the file is read as if it was being input from the keyboard, hence the use of the word **INPUT**. Because the file is read sequentially from start to finish there has to be some mechanism that tells the program that the last record in the file has been read. This is an end-of-file marker and this is known as **EOF(n)** where **n** is the channel number of the file. The program is made constantly to look for this. Then the records are read using a statement such as

INPUT#1, variable names

The program is shown in Fig. 5.5.

Fig 5.5

```
10 OPEN "I",1,"Names"
20 IF EOF(1) THEN STOP
30 WHILE NOT(EOF(1))
40 INPUT#1,A$,B$,C$,D$,E$,F$
50 PRINT B$+" "+A$
60 PRINT C$
```

58

```
70 PRINT D$
80 PRINT E$
90 PRINT F$
100 PRINT
110 WEND
```

Program outline: The statement on line 10 opens the file for reading (input) and line 20 contains the instruction on what to do when the end-of-file marker is detected. Note that the instruction says WHILE NOT(EOF(1)) . . . This uses the word NOT to negate a truth. One could write WHILE A=B which means while the statement that A=B is true. WHILE NOT(A=B) means while A is not equal to B. So WHILE NOT(EOF(1)) means while no end-of-file is detected or "until an end-of-file is detected". Six records are read in and displayed on the screen so that the title and initials are displayed separated from the surname by a space and the rest of the address underneath. You should notice that the structure of both these programs is very similar.

The program that extracts data from the file assumes that the file already exists. The program that writes data to the file will create a new file every time it runs so there has to be an instruction that stops this happening if you merely wish to add extra data onto the end of an existing file. To do this we open the file in "Append" mode and the first statement in the program would then be

OPEN "A",1,"Names" .

so that all the data is added onto the end of an existing file called **Names** which would have its data stored so that part of it looks like this:

```
"Harris","Ms J","34 Ramsey St","Melbourne","NSW","ML7 6YT"
"Jimson","Mr T","23 Railway Cuttings","East Cheam","Surrey","GL7 6TR"
```

When the second program displays the result on the screen they will look as shown in Fig.5.6.

Fig 5.6

```
Ms J Harris
34 Ramsey St
Melbourne
NSW
ML7 6YT
```

Mr T Jimson
23 Railway Cuttings
East Cheam
Surrey
GL7 6TR

Now it may be that you wish to interrogate the file and discover the address of a particular person. In order to do this the file has to be searched on what is called a "key". In this case the key will be the surname of the person. The file is searched from start to finish until the correct key is found and the address displayed. The program to do this is shown in Fig. 5.7.

Fig 5.7

```
10 OPEN "I",1,"Names"
20 INPUT "Surname to be searched for ";T$
30 WHILE NOT(EOF(1))
40 INPUT#1,A$,B$,C$,D$,E$,F$
50 IF T$=A$ THEN PRINT B$+" "+A$:PRINT C$:PRINT D$:PRINT E$:PRINT
F$:STOP:CLOSE#1
60 WEND
70 PRINT "Surname not found"
```

Program outline: This program starts by opening the file for input to the machine. The required key is requested and a similar loop is traversed as before. However, only when the name input matches exactly the string A$ does the address get displayed. If the end of the file is reached without a match being found then the "Not found" message is displayed. Notice that the file is closed off by the CLOSE#1 statement at the end of line 50. If the end of the file is reached then it is automatically closed.

A program that modifies the contents of a file tends to be more complicated that the ones demonstrated previously. Such a program requires the use of *two files* since the technique is to copy all the records up to the one to be modified onto another file, then the modification is placed on the next record of the new file and finally the rest of the file is copied across record by record. The program that will do this is shown in Fig. 5.8

Fig 5.8

```
10 OPEN "I",1,"Names"
15 OPEN "O",2,"Newnames"
20 INPUT "Surname to be searched for ";T$
30 WHILE NOT(EOF(1))
```

```
40 INPUT#1,A$,B$,C$,D$,E$,F$
50 IF T$=A$ THEN PRINT B$+" "+A$:PRINT C$:PRINT D$:PRINT E$:PRINT
   F$:INPUT  "New  street";C$:INPUT  "New  town";D$:INPUT  "New
   county";E$:INPUT "New postcode";F$
55 WRITE#2,A$,B$,C$,D$,E$,F$
60 WEND
65 CLOSE#1
66 CLOSE#2
70 KILL "Names"
80 NAME "Newnames" AS "Names"
```

**Program outline: First of all two files are open file #1 for
reading (input) and file #2 for output (writing). After the
surname has been requested the file is searched record by
record until a match is found. If no match is found then
the name and address is written onto the new file. If a
match is found then the new address details are requested
and these are written to the new file. Notice how both
options use the same line to write to the file - line 55.
After all the file details have been written across both of
the files are closed and line 70 deletes the original file
called "Names" and line 80 renames the new file with the
old name, so that it can be read by the program in Fig. 5.5.**

5.4 FILES IN DATA PROCESSING

The kind of data for which a serial file would be used
would be for such things as updating a name and address
file as shown already, or possibly even for maintaining a
stock file. The usual way, of course, would not be to make
amendments one at a time but to amend a whole series of
records. The amendments would be batched together into a
file and the amendments file merged with the existing file
in order to produce a new updated file. In practice this is
a very useful method of operation since a hierarchy of
files is created forming a "grandparent", "parent" and
"child" set of files. The procedure for creating a new
updated file is shown in Fig. 5.9. By following this
sequence of events the carried-forward file for this week
becomes the brought-forward file for next week, and so on.
By having this hierarchy of files it is possible to recreate
a file by re-running the update program should any failure
take place. It is for this reason that there is a need for
librarians to take charge of the disk and tape files in a
large computer centre.

The procedure to update, say, a stock file is first of all
to collect the changes which are to be made to the file
(that is, the issues of stock, arrival of new stock and the
insertion of new stock items into the file). The data

relating to all these will arrive during, say, a week and in a haphazard order. This data is then collected into a file and validated in order to prevent any unacceptable data being processed. For example, invalid dates such as 31st February would be rejected. In addition, part numbers are often made up in such a way as to contain inbuilt checks as in the Standard Book Number allocated to every book published. These numbers all have to be checked. (Remember that **Garbage In results in Garbage Out.**) Checks are thus made for every possible type of error in the data in order to prevent the program trying to process rubbish. Once the data has been validated it needs to be sorted into some kind of order. This order is dictated by the order of data on the *file being updated*. If the main file is in part number order then the data used to amend it must also be in that order. The two files can then to be merged and a new updated file created. Even at the merging process errors can be detected. These are known as *reconciliation errors*. These occur when additional stock is bought for a part that is not yet on file, or when stock of a discontinued line has apparently been issued. The retention of the original stock file and the new, updated, file is obviously important so that these reconciliation errors can be put right.

Fig 5.9 *Flowchart for updated file*

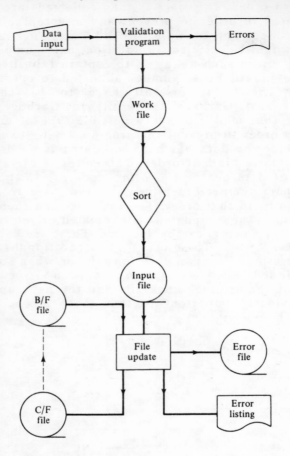

A flowchart for the merging of two files is shown in Fig. 5.10 and the program which will effect this is shown in Fig. 5.11. The files are already sorted into key order, the key being the number that is the first field in each record. Notice that when the program discovers that the end of each file has been reached the key is set to 99999. Fig. 5.12 shows the result of running the program.

Fig 5.10 *Flowchart for merging two files*

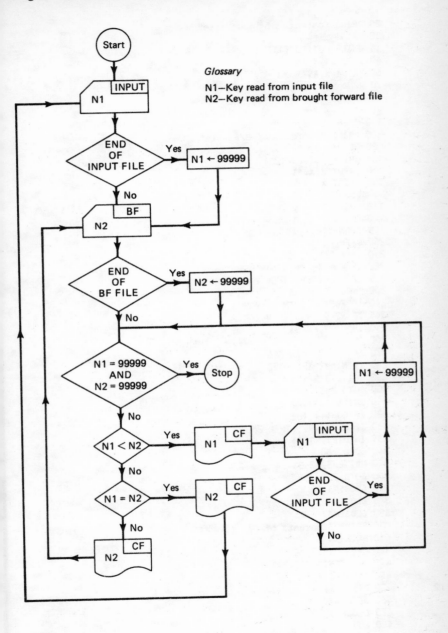

Glossary

N1—Key read from input file
N2—Key read from brought forward file

64

Fig 5.11

```
10 OPEN "I",1,"Input"
20 PRINT"Contents of input file"
30 PRINT
35 WHILE NOT(EOF(1))
40 INPUT#1,X,A$
60 PRINT X,A$
70 WEND
80 CLOSE#1
90 PRINT
100 OPEN "I",2,"BF"
110 PRINT "Contents of B/F file"
120 PRINT
125 WHILE NOT(EOF(2))
130 INPUT#2,X,A$
150 PRINT X,A$
160 WEND
170 CLOSE#2
180 PRINT
190 OPEN "I",1,"Input"
200 OPEN "I",2,"BF"
210 OPEN "O",3,"CF"
220 IF EOF(1) THEN N1=99999!
225 IF N1=99999! THEN 240
230 INPUT#1,N1,A$
240 IF EOF(2) THEN N2=99999!
245 IF N2=99999! THEN 260
250 INPUT#2,N2,B$
260 IF N1=99999! AND N2=99999! THEN 370
270 IF N1<N2 THEN 310
280 IF N1=N2 THEN 350
290 WRITE#3,N2,B$
300 GOTO 240
310 WRITE#3,N1,A$
320 IF EOF(1) THEN N1=99999!
330 IF N1=99999! THEN 260
335 INPUT#1,N1,A$
340 GOTO 260
350 WRITE#3,N2,B$
360 GOTO 230
370 CLOSE#1
380 CLOSE#2
390 CLOSE#3
400 PRINT "Contents of C/F file"
410 PRINT
420 OPEN "I",3,"CF"
425 WHILE NOT(EOF(3))
430 INPUT#3,X,A$
450 PRINT X,A$
460 WEND
470 CLOSE#3
480 END
```

Fig 5.12 *Result of running the program in Fig. 5.11*

Contents of input file

2341	P.JONES
2546	J.SMITH
3345	K.WILLIAMS
4421	L.POPPLE
4567	W.WINN
5501	T.SERGEANT
5678	O.PEASGOOD
5782	O.ROBSON
6671	D.WARD
6672	P.WATSON
7708	D.KNIGHT

Contents of B/F file

2314	H.BROWN
2455	T.WATSON
3321	J.HUNT
3451	P.WILLIAMS
3555	H.PYM
3675	M.THATCHER
4091	M.FOOT
4213	P.SCOTT
4561	T.JACKSON
5467	F.BOGG
5560	H.SECOMBE
5789	S.MILLIGAN
6601	R.TWELVETREE
6608	T.HOOD
7701	T.COPPLE

Contents of C/F file

2314	H.BROWN
2341	P.JONES
2455	T.WATSON
2546	J.SMITH
3321	J.HUNT
3345	K.WILLIAMS
3451	P.WILLIAMS
3555	H.PYM
3675	M.THATCHER
4091	M.FOOT
4213	P.SCOTT
4421	L.POPPLE
4561	T.JACKSON
4567	W.WINN
5467	F.BOGG
5501	T.SERGEANT
5560	H.SECOMBE
5678	O.PEASGOOD
5782	O.ROBSON
5789	S.MILLIGAN
6601	R.TWELVETREE
6608	T.HOOD
6671	D.WARD
6672	P.WATSON
7701	T.COPPLE
7708	D.KNIGHT

5.5 RANDOM ACCESS FILES

Finally a word about random access files, or "direct access files", as they are sometimes called. With files of this type it is necessary to specify only the number of the record within the file for it to be accessed directly instead of having all the records preceding it read first. This is because when a record is written in to a random file not only are the contents of the record specified but also the number of the record. In other words it is rather like saying "put this data on page 34 of the ledger" rather than "put this data on the next available page of the ledger".

A serial file is opened for writing to with an instruction such as

        OPEN "O",1,"FILENAME"

and for writing with an instruction like

        OPEN "I",1,"FILENAME"

A random file is opened for both reading and writing with an instruction such as

        OPEN "R",1,"FILENAME"

All data stored in a random file is stored in *string form* so that every piece of data must be converted into a string. This means that if you want to store integers, single precision numbers or double precision numbers you need to use the functions

MKI$	Convert an integer into a 2-byte string
MKS$	Convert a single precision number into a 4-byte string
MKD$	Convert a double precision number into an 8-byte string

The entries are converted back from strings to numbers by using the following functions

CVI	Converts the string to an integer
CVS	Converts the string to a single precision number

| CVD | Converts the string to a double precision number |

In addition, each string record must be set to the left or right of the field allotted to it by using

| LSET | Place the string to the left of the field |
| RSET | Place the string to the right of the field |

After the file has been opened its structure must be specified so that the statement to follow the **OPEN** statement must be of the form

FIELD 1, 10 AS A\$,20 AS B\$,4 AS C\$

meaning that each record consists of three fields; 10 bytes for the variable called **A\$**, 20 bytes for the variable called **B\$** and four for the variable **C\$**.

Writing to a record in the file is effected by the instruction

PUT 1,REC

where **REC** is the record number written to; the record is retrieved by the instruction

GET 1,REC

The next example illustrates the creation and reading of a random access file. It is to be a file that contains telephone numbers and names of companies. The first record on the file will contain a single number that tells us the number of the next record to be filled. After that the records consist of a pair of fields, the first giving the phone number and the second giving the name of the company. But first of all we have to initialise the first record on the file and this is done with the small program shown in Fig. 5.13.

Fig 5.13

```
10 OPEN "R",1,"Phones"
20 FIELD 1,20 AS N$,20 AS N1$
30 N=2
40 LSET N$=MKI$(N)
50 PUT 1,1
60 CLOSE
```

Program outline: A random access file called "Phones" is opened with two fields per record, although only one of them is going to be used. The variable N is set to the value of 2 put into the first record of the file. This number will be the number of the first record available for data when the next program is run. This because in this file the first record is occupied by a number that tells the program the record number of the next number to be filled when the file is updated.

Then the next program reads records into the file. It is shown in Fig.5.14.

Fig 5.14

```
10 OPEN "R",1,"Phones"
50 FIELD 1, 20 AS F1$,20 AS F2$
55 GET 1,1
56 REC=CVI(F1$)
70 INPUT "Phone number:";P$
80 IF P$="0" THEN GOTO 170
90 INPUT "Name:";N$
100 LSET F1$=P$
110 LSET F2$=N$
120 PUT 1,REC
130 PRINT REC
140 REC=REC+1
150 GOTO 70
170 LSET F1$=MKI$(REC)
180 PUT 1,1
190 PRINT REC
200 CLOSE#1
```

Program outline: First of all the file is opened and the fields defined, as in Fig. 5.13. The number of the next record to be filled is already on the file. It is read as a string and converted to a number on lines 55 and 56. Then the fields are read in from the keyboard and placed in successive records and the number in REC is continually updated. When input is terminated by entering a trigger value for P$, the last value of REC is read into the first record. It will be the number of the next available record when the program is run again.

In order to read the data from the file the program shown in Fig. 5.15 is used.

Fig 5.15

```
10 OPEN "R",1,"Phones"
50 FIELD 1,20 AS N1$, 20 AS N2$
55 GET 1,1
56 N=CVI(N1$)
60 FOR K=2 TO N-1
70 GET 1,K
80 PRINT N1$,N2$
90 NEXT K
```

Program outline: This program reads the value of N from the first record in the file and then uses it in a loop to read the records that exist. Remember that N is one less than the number of records on the file and that the first record does not contain the data we want listing. This is why we read from the second record onwards.

Now that we have a random access file we can proceed to do things with it. For example, we can sort it into some sort of order. The next example - Fig. 5.16 - shows how we can use the bubble sort technique on the contents of a random access file. In the same way as the numbers or names in a list can be moved about during the sorting process we can move records in the file about to achieve the same result.

Fig 5.16

```
10 OPEN "R",1,"Phones"
20 FIELD 1, 20 AS F1$,20 AS F2$
30 GET 1,1
40 J=CVI(F1$)
50 N=J
60 K=0
70 J=J-1
80 FOR I= 2 TO J-1
90 GET 1,I:A1$=F1$:A2$=F2$
100 GET 1,I+1:B1$=F1$:B2$=F2$
110 IF A2$>B2$ THEN 150
120 NEXT I
130 IF K=0 THEN 210
140 GOTO 60
150 LSET F1$=B1$:LSET F2$=B2$
160 PUT 1,I
```

```
170 LSET F1$=A1$:LSET F2$=A2$
180 PUT 1,I+1
190 K=1
200 GOTO 120
210 FOR I=2 TO N-1
220 PRINT I;
230 GET 1,I
240 PRINT F1$;":";F2$
250 NEXT I
260 STOP
270 CLOSE#1
```

Program outline: First of all the number of the next available record is read from the first record of the file. This will, of course, be two less than the number of usable records on the file. Then a bubble sort takes place with the testing taking place in line 110 and the swapping taking place in lines 150 to 180. It is not a simple "swap" this time. All that is done is that the records are re-written into each other's locations on the disk. Finally the sorted list is produced with the individual record numbers beside the output to show the new locations of the data.

As a general rule it should be noted that if a file is *opened* as a serial file it can be *accessed* only as a serial file. A file opened as a random file must always be treated as a random file. The example program shown in Fig. 5.17 shows how we can compute the record number from a numeric key, in this case a four-digit telephone number. The technique is that of *hash coding* where the record number to be allocated to a particular record is found by some arithmetic operation performed on the key to that record. In this example the first two digits of the key are divided by two. This gives the record number for that record. If there is data already stored there then the next in order is used. If that is occupied then next is tried, and so on. The formula for calculating the record number must bear some relation to the number of records likely to be placed on the file. In this case, for practicability, only fifty records are used.

The program shown in Fig. 5.18 shows how any record can be found in the file by recalculating the record number to be searched for from its key. The amount of searching through the file is minimised by this method, so all that is needed is to type in the telephone number and the name associated with that number is quickly found. Fig. 5.19 shows a list of the contents of the file. Chapter 8 contains some more examples of the use of random access files.

Fig 5.17

```
10 OPEN "R",1,"Nofile"
20 FIELD 1,2 AS N1$,10 AS N2$
30 LSET N1$=MKI$(-1):LSET N2$=MKI$(0)
40 FOR I = 1 TO 50
50 PUT 1,I
60 NEXT I
70 FOR J=1 TO 50
80 INPUT A$,B$
90 IF A$="0" THEN STOP:CLOSE#1
100 K=VAL(A$)/100
110 K=INT(K/2)
120 GET 1,K
130 IF CVI(N1$)=-1 THEN LSET N1$=MKI$(VAL(A$)):LSET N2$=B$:PUT
1,K:GOTO 170
140 K=K+1
150 IF K>50 THEN K=1
160 GOTO 120
170 NEXT J
```

Program outline: The first thing performed by this program is to fill each record with a -1 and a zero as dummy data. Then pairs of names and numbers are placed on the file according to the rule that divides the number by 100 and then takes the whole number part of the result. This gives the record number for that record. If the record is occupied then next one is tried. This continues until the first unoccupied record is found. If Record 50 is occupied then Record 1 is tried.

Fig 5.18

```
10 OPEN "R",1,"Nofile"
20 FIELD 1,2 AS N1$,10 AS N2$
30 INPUT "Number to be searched for"; N$
40 R=0
50 IF N$="END" THEN STOP:CLOSE#1
60 K=INT(VAL(N$)/100)/2
70 GET 1,K
80 R=R+1
90 IF VAL(N$)=CVI(N1$) THEN PRINT CVI(N1$),N2$:GOTO 30
100 K=K+1
110 IF R=50 THEN 140
120 IF K>50 THEN K=1
130 GOTO 70
140 CLOSE#1
150 PRINT"Number not found"
160 GOTO 30
```

Program outline: This program will search for a record in the file using the same technique to search as was used to allot the record numbers in the program in Fig. 5.17. The variable R is used as a flag to tell the program how many records have been tested. As there are only 50 records in this file the test in line 110 tells the program that every record has been tested and no match has been found.

Fig 5.19 *The contents of the file after a number of records have been stored*

```
 1  -1
 2  -1
 3  -1
 4  -1
 5  -1
 6  -1
 7  -1
 8  1679      WALTERS
 9  -1
10  2134      MORTON
11  2345      SMITH
12  2223      THOMPSON
13  2346      BROADWAY
14  -1
15  -1
16  -1
17  -1
18  -1
19  -1
20  -1
21  -1
22  -1
23  -1
24  -1
25  -1
26  -1
27  -1
28  -1
29  -1
30  -1
31  -1
32  -1
33  -1
34  -1
35  -1
36  -1
37  -1
38  -1
39  -1
40  -1
41  -1
42  -1
43  -1
44  8852      LOCKWOOD
45  9021      ROCHESTER
46  8832      CRACKNELL
47  9055      BLYTON
48  8875      COON
49  9901      FINCH
50  9821      MAYWOOD
```

SUBROUTINES

6.1 A MUSICAL DIGRESSION

The first Noël: A Christmas Carol

The first Noël the angels did say
was to certain poor shepherds in fields where they lay
In fields where they lay keeping their sheep
on a cold winter's night that was so deep.

GOTO CHORUS

They looked up and saw a star
shining in the East beyond them far.
And to the Earth it gave great light
and so it continued both day and night.

GOTO CHORUS

The star it shone from the North-West
O'er Bethlehem it took its rest.
And there it did both stop and stay
right over the place where Jesus lay.

GOTO CHORUS

And by the light of that same star
three wise men came from country far.
To seek for a king was their intent
And to follow the star wherever it went.

GOTO CHORUS

STOP

CHORUS

Noël, Noël, Noël, Noël. Born is the King of Israel.

RETURN

Soldier, Soldier Won't you marry me?
American / English Folk Song

Soldier, soldier won't you marry me,
With your musket, fife and drum?
How can I marry such a pretty maid, when I have
no shoes to put on?

GOTO CHORUS (Cobbler's)

Soldier, soldier won't you marry me,
With your musket, fife and drum?
How can I marry such a pretty maid, when I have
no socks to put on?

GOTO CHORUS (Draper's)

Soldier, soldier won't you marry me,
With your musket, fife and drum?
How can I marry such a pretty maid, when I have
no pants to put on?

GOTO CHORUS (Tailor's)

Soldier, soldier won't you marry me,
With your musket, fife and drum?
How can I marry such a pretty maid, when I've
a wife and baby at home?

STOP

CHORUS(shop)

Off to the shop she did go as fast as she could run,
Brought back the finest was there and the soldier
put them on.

RETURN

It might seem incongruous at first sight to include a Christmas carol and a folk song in a book on computer programming. However, close inspection of the words of the songs show that they are not quite written in the conventional manner. Look at the way the choruses are written down. In the carol we see that GOTO CHORUS is printed and at the end of the chorus, which is written separately from the main body of the carol, the word RETURN appears. The chorus of a song is, in fact, a common use of what in computing is called a *subroutine*. A subroutine is a temporary deviation from the main theme of what is going on in the (in this case) song with a return to the point where the deviation took place. In the first case we have a chorus which is exactly the same each time. In the second example, the folk song, the main body of the chorus remains the same but a different word is inserted into the space provided for it. The first time the chorus is sung we put the word "cobbler's" in. The second time round we insert the word "draper's" and so on. This means that although the main part of the chorus is the same each time its meaning is altered by the inclusion of a particular word. The word is specified at the appropriate point in the verse when the chorus is brought in, thus adding to the narrative of the song.

6.2 DOWN TO BUSINESS

A subroutine in a computer program is very like the chorus of a song. When the time is right we leave the main body of the program and go to a *subordinate part* of the program which performs some frequently required function. As with the song chorus we need to write this subordinate part out only once and refer to it whenever necessary. Most subroutines work in the way that the chorus of the folk song works. We hand over a number, or a set of numbers, to the subroutine so that it can process them in its own way and then hand back control to the main program. A very simple example of this has already been used when, in a BASIC program, we need to calculate the square root of a number. We do not need to tell the computer how to calculate square roots every time we need to perform the calculation. All that is needed is to use the keyword SQR followed by whatever variable we wish to have rooted and then leave it alone. The computer software contains a special square root subprogram which handles the calculation and hands the answer back to the program which had called for it. If we write a program starting off with the lines

```
10  INPUT X
20  Y = SQR(X)
30  PRINT Y
    .
    .
    .
```

then at line 20 the calculation of the square root is handed over to a software routine which will work out the square root of the variable X and then hand the answer back to the program ready for it to be allocated to the variable Y.

There are a number of these functions available in all versions of BASIC. They are all characterised by having a single variable name enclosed in the brackets following the function name, although this could be a complex expression such as

$$SQR(B^2-4*A*C)$$

This expression is known as the *argument* so that if an attempt is made to evaluate the square root of a negative number then a message such as

ERROR - INVALID ARGUMENT

will be displayed indicating that the subroutine cannot cope with the data it has been handed.

Some other functions used in programs so far are:

VAL - used to return the numeric value of a string of numerals

TAB - positions the cursor or the printing head of your printer

SPC - leave a number of spaces

Any reader who wishes to use BASIC seriously should consult the manufacturer's handbook for a full list of the functions available for that particular version of the language.

6.3 HOME-MADE FUNCTIONS

BASIC allows the programmer to *write his own functions* by defining them at the start of the program by using

DEF FNa(X)

where **a** is any letter of the alphabet and **X** is the subroutine argument. For example

10 DEF FNA(X)=3*x^2+2*x-3

means that the function subroutine defined above will always refer to the value of $3x^2 + 2x - 3$ whenever FNA is used in the program. An example of a home-made function (two, in fact) is found in the program shown in Fig. 6.1. This program is used to line up numbers so that they are printed with the decimal points lying under one another, something which BASIC does not do very well without help. Notice also the number of other functions used in this program.

Fig 6.1

```
10 DEF FNT(N)=INT(LOG(ABS(N))/LOG(10))
20 DEF FNS(N)=INT(LOG(.1+ABS(N))/LOG(10))
30 READ N
40 IF N=0 THEN 140
50 T=10
60 IF ABS(N)<.1 THEN 90
70 PRINT TAB(T-FNT(N));N
80 GOTO 30
90 PRINT TAB(T-FNS(N));N
100 GOTO 30
110 DATA 3.45,56.7,789.05,-67.8,54,-1.0005,45.567,-45.567
120 DATA 0.3,-0.008,45,467.89,.1,99999,2,3,-1
130 DATA 0
140 STOP
```

Program outline: For the non-mathematical reader, the exact calculations performed by the functions defined in lines 10 and 20 will not be analysed. Suffice it to say that two fairly complicated mathematical calculations are defined by the two functions called FNT and FNS, and these are called on lines 70 and 90. Line 30 contains an alternative to INPUT and sends the program to seek for data on special DATA lines, lines 110,120 and 130 in this case. The first time line 10 is executed N is assigned the value of 3.45, then this number is processed and printed in line 90. Line 100 sends the program back to line 30 where the next number on the DATA line is read and assigned to N, 56.7 this time. This loop continues until N is assigned the last value on the DATA list, 0, which acts as a trigger to stop the program. Should there be no command of this sort then the program will continue to try to read data which does not exist and give you a message such as

OUT OF DATA IN LINE 120

and the program would stop - a very inelegant way of stopping a program.

6.4 BASIC SUBROUTINES

If subroutines longer than one line are required by a BASIC program then the words **GOSUB** and **RETURN** are used. In this case the subroutine is a special part of the program containing the instructions that make up the subroutine, and this is entered by writing

GOSUB 2000

for example. This instructs the program to go immediately to line 2000 and continue from that point until the instruction

RETURN

is encountered. This signifies the end of the subroutine and the program jumps back to the line immediately following the GOSUB last executed. A very simple example of this in action is shown in Fig. 6.2. A far more meaningful use of a subroutine is shown in Fig. 6.3 where the subroutine is used to check the validity of a book number. Only part of the complete program is shown as it is a section of a book-issuing system for a library. The validity of a book number must be checked before the details of its issue are placed on a file.

Fig 6.2

```
10 PRINT"Start of program"
20 GOSUB 100
30 PRINT"I'm at line 30"
40 GOSUB 200
50 PRINT"I'm at line 50"
60 GOSUB 100
70 PRINT"This is the end"
80 STOP
100 REM***SUBROUTINE NO.1***
110 PRINT"I'm in the first subroutine"
120 PRINT"I'm at line 120"
130 RETURN
200 REM***SUBROUTINE NO.2***
210 PRINT"I'm in the second subroutine now!"
220 PRINT"I'm at line 220"
230 RETURN
240 END
```

Program outline: The first line will print the heading "Start of program", then line 20 will cause a jump to line 100 so that lines 110 and 120 are executed. The instruction on line 130 will send the program back to the line immediately following the instruction which sent the program off to the subroutine, line 30. Then line 30 is executed and line 40 sends the program off to the subroutine which starts at line 200. Then lines 210 and 220 are executed and line 230 sends the program back to line 70. Then the first subroutine is executed again but this time the return is to line 70. Then the program stops. The sequence of line numbers executed by this program will therefore be 10, 20, 100, 110, 120, 130, 30, 40, 200, 210, 220, 230, 50, 60, 100, 110, 120, 130, 70, 80.

Fig 6.3

```
5 REM***PART OF A BOOK ISSUING SYSTEM***
10 OPEN "A",1,"Workfile"
20 INPUT "Date: DD/MM/YY"; D$
30 INPUT "Book ISBN:";ISBN$
40 IF ISBN$="END" THEN CLOSE#1: STOP
44 INPUT "Issue or Return I/R:";I$
45 GOSUB 1000
50 IF VALID$="Yes" THEN WRITE#1,D$,ISBN$,I$ ELSE PRINT"Invalid
ISBN - try again":GOTO 30
70 GOTO 30
999 STOP
1000 VALID$="No"
1010 IF LEN(ISBN$)<>10 THEN PRINT "Invalid ISBN":STOP
1020 TOTAL=0
1030 NUMBER=10
```

```
1030 NUMBER=10
1040 FOR COUNT=1 TO 9
1050 AMOUNT=VAL(MID$(ISBN$,COUNT,1))
1060 TOTAL=TOTAL+NUMBER*AMOUNT
1070 NUMBER=NUMBER-1
1080 NEXT COUNT
1090    IF    RIGHT$(ISBN$,1)="X"    THEN    AMOUNT=10    ELSE
AMOUNT=VAL(RIGHT$(ISBN$,1))
1100 TOTAL=TOTAL+NUMBER*AMOUNT
1110 IF TOTAL/11=INT(TOTAL/11) THEN VALID$="Yes"
1120 RETURN
```

Program outline: A workfile is opened first of all, in Append Mode, thus enabling data to be written on to the end of an existing serial file. First of all the date is entered followed by the book ISBN. This then causes a jump to the subroutine that validates the book number and returns a variable called VALID$ that can be either "Yes" or "No". The validation in the subroutine depends on the fact the ISBN for every book is unique and must consist of 10 characters of which the first nine are digits and the last one, a check digit, is either a number in the range 1 through 9 or the letter X. The checking of the number is performed by a simple rule. The first digit is multiplied by 10, the second by 9, the third by 8 and so on until the ninth digit is multiplied by 1 and these sums are added together. Then the last digit is added in to the total and if this is the letter X then 10 is added to the total. The result must be exactly divisible by 11. If it is not then the ISBN is invalid. Only when a valid book number is entered is the date, ISBN and a record of it being issued or withdrawn is placed on the file.

6.5 CALLED SUBROUTINES

All versions of BASIC allow subroutines to be incorporated into a program as shown in the previous section. This does not make BASIC an economical language to use. These subroutines tend to make conventional BASIC programs rather lengthy and complicated, and hence difficult to follow. All the other high-level languages we meet in later chapters will allow us to create separate subroutines as separate entities which are called on whenever required, just like the chorus of a song. Nevertheless some of the techniques of using subroutines can be described using BASIC, as the next example will show. It demonstrates the method of *passing parameters* between the main program and the subroutine. The program is listed in Fig. 6.4.

Fig 6.4

```
10 INPUT A,B,C
20 IF A>B THEN 70
30 IF B>C THEN 130
40 IF A>B THEN 190
50 PRINT "The numbers in order are:";A;B;C
60 STOP
70 X=A
80 Y=B
90 GOSUB 250
100 A=X
110 B=Y
120 GOTO 30
130 X=B
140 Y=C
150 GOSUB 250
160 B=X
170 C=Y
180 GOTO 40
190 X=A
200 Y=B
210 GOSUB 250
220 A=X
230 B=Y
240 GOTO 50
250 REM***SWAP SUBROUTINE***
260 SWAP X,Y
270 RETURN
```

Program outline: The test of pairs of numbers are in lines 20 to 40 and the result is printed at line 50. The subroutine is kept in lines 250 to 270 and you will notice that it knows about only two variables, X and Y. This means that before the subroutine is entered the first time the values of A and B are passed to X and Y. These two variables are swapped over and on the return at lines 100 and 110 A and B are given the swapped values. Then next time the subroutine is executed X and Y are given the values belonging to B and C. X and Y are swapped over and then on return the new values are passed back to B and C. Finally the same thing takes place with A and B again. X and Y are the "parameters" of the subroutine and values are passed to them to process and then the results are passed back to the main program.

Fig. 6.5 shows a program that merges the contents of two sorted lists into a third sorted list. It uses two subroutines, called **GETNEXT** and **ADD** respectively. The first of these gets the next number from one of the original lists A and

B. The subroutine **ADD** adds the appropriate number into its proper place in the final list C.

Fig 6.5

```
10 DIM A(100),B(100),C(100),X(200)
20 INPUT "List A - How many numbers ";N1
30 FOR I = 1 TO N1
40 INPUT A(I)
50 NEXT I
60 INPUT "List B - How many numbers ";N2
70 FOR I = 1 TO N2
80 INPUT B(I)
90 NEXT I
100 P=A(1)
110 Q=B(1)
120 L=2
130 K=1
140 J=2
150 IF P<Q THEN 350
160 H=Q
170 GOSUB 660
180 M=J
190 X(M)=B(M)
200 N=N2
210 GOSUB 580
220 Q=H
230 J=M
240 IF E<>1 THEN 150
250 H=P
260 GOSUB 660
270 M=L
280 X(M)=A(M)
290 N=N1
300 GOSUB 580
310 P=H
320 L=M
330 IF E=1 THEN 540
340 GOTO 250
350 H=P
360 GOSUB 660
370 M=L
380 X(M)=A(M)
390 N=N1
400 GOSUB 580
410 P=H
420 L=M
430 IF E<>1 THEN 150
440 H=Q
```

```
450 GOSUB 660
460 M=J
470 X(M)=B(M)
480 N=N2
490 GOSUB 580
500 J=M
510 Q=H
520 IF E=1 THEN 540
530 GOTO 440
535 PRINT"Final merged list"
540 FOR I = 1 TO K-1
550 PRINT C(I)
560 NEXT I
570 STOP
580 REM***GETNEXT***
590 E=0
600 IF M>N THEN 640
610 H=X(M)
620 M=M+1
630 GOTO 650
640 E=1
650 RETURN
660 REM***ADD***
670 C(K)=H
680 K=K+1
690 RETURN
700 END
```

Program outline: First of all the numbers in the lists A and B are input. They must be in ascending numerical order otherwise the program will not work. The final list containing the merged list in ascending order is the list C. The next thing to happen is that the first number in A is assigned to the variable P and the first number in B is assigned to the variable Q - lines 100 and 110. The variables L and J keep track of the next number to be read from lists A and B. The variable K keeps track of the next number to be written into the list C. This means that by the time line 150 has been reached the next numbers to be read from lists A and B are the second in each case and the first number has yet to be written into list C. If the value of P is less than the value of Q then it P that is written into list C thus calling for the ADD subroutine which will make P the Kth element of that list and increases K by 1. After ADD has been executed we have to get the next number from list A, which is what the GETNEXT subroutine is for, and allocate that value to P.

Then we go back to line 150 again. The variable E is a flag which tells the program that the end of one of the lists has been reached. This will cause all that remains of the other list to be written into list C until that produces another flag to denote the end of that list. Finally the list C is displayed and the program ends. The list called X is the only list known to the GETNEXT subroutine and so it is necessary to allocate the Mth element of list B to the Mth element of X in line 190 and similarly in lines 280, 380 and 470.

GRAPHICS IN BASIC

7.1 INTRODUCTION

BASIC provides you with a number of commands that will enable you to produce graphics on the screen of your PC. The results you get depend to a large extent on the type of screen you have; colour or monochrome, high resolution or low resolution. This means that the contents of this chapter will not be "all you need to know about graphics via BASIC", but rather just an overview of the types of things you can do.

First of all you should be able to examine the capabilities of your screen by using the **SCREEN** command. This is a command that you can place in a program wherever you wish so that you can define the quality of the graphics you produce. There are basically four modes applicable to this command:

SCREEN 0	Text mode
SCREEN 1	Medium Resolution graphics mode
SCREEN 2	High Resolution graphics mode
SCREEN 3	Super-High Resolution graphics mode

In fact for the last of these the argument (the number following the command) can be in the range 3 to 255.

Text Mode	Monochrome text mode giving 80 columns by 25 rows

Medium Res.	Colour (four different colours available) text giving 40 columns by 25 rows and the screen divided into 320 horizontal pixels and 200 vertical pixels
High Res.	Monochrome high resolution graphics 640 horizontal pixels and 200 vertical pixels. 80 columns and 25 rows for text
Super-High Res.	Monochrome high resolution graphics 640 horizontal pixels and 400 vertical pixels; 80 columns and 25 rows for text (Not available on all PCs, it depends on the hardware)

A *pixel* is a "picture cell" and is the units of resolution on a screen. The more pixels to the square inch, the higher the definition.

7.2 LINE AND BOX DRAWING

The position of a pixel on your screen is defined by a pair of coordinates, X and Y, where the top left-hand corner of the screen has coordinates (0,0) and the bottom right-hand corner has coordinates (319,199) in medium resolution mode, (619,179) in high resolution mode and (619,399) in super-high resolution mode. This "upside-down" way of expressing a position can be confusing to mathematicians, who expect things to be the other way up.

In order to draw a line all that is needed is the command **LINE**. It can be used in several ways. For example

    LINE(0,0)-(639,199)

will draw a line for the top left-hand corner of the screen to the bottom right-hand corner in High Resolution mode. The command

    LINE-(639,199)

will draw a line from the last point referenced to the bottom right-hand corner of a high resolution screen. The **LINE** command is used in the program shown in Fig. 7.1.

Fig 7.1

```
10 CLS
20 SCREEN 2
30 LINE(19,19)-(19,179)
40 LINE,-(619,179)
50 LINE-(619,19)
60 LINE -(19,19)
```

Program outline: The first line of the program uses the command CLS to clear the screen. Then the screen is set to high resolution graphics mode and a line is drawn from the top left-hand corner to the top right-hand corner. Then to the bottom right-hand corner, the bottom left-hand corner and finally back to the top left-hand corner again. In fact the box that is drawn is set in from each corner for a reason that will appear later.

The screen that you see after running that program is shown in Fig. 7.2.

Fig. 7.2 *Screen following from running program in Fig. 7.1*

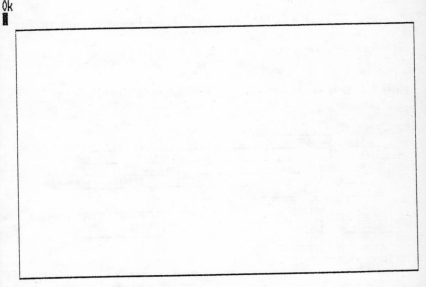

The next program illustrated in Fig. 7.3 takes the use of **LINE** a little further so that a set of grids are drawn on the screen.

Fig 7.3

```
10 CLS
20 SCREEN 2
30 LINE(19,19)-(619,179),,B
70 FOR COL = 29 TO 619 STEP 10
80 LINE(COL,19)-(COL,179)
90 NEXT COL
100 FOR ROW = 29 TO 179 STEP 10
110 LINE(19,ROW)-(619,ROW)
120 NEXT ROW
```

Program outline: This program draws a series of grid lines within a box both horizontally and vertically at intervals of ten pixels. The command on line 30 is a shortened version of the program in Fig. 7.1. By defining the top left-hand corner and the bottom right-hand corner of your box in a LINE command and adding the B qualifier - separated by two commas - the box is drawn by one command rather than four. The next step is to draw the vertical grid lines at ten-pixel intervals by the loop in lines 70 to 90. A similar thing is done for the horizontal grid lines, again at ten-pixel intervals, in lines 100 to 120.

The screen that you get after running the program in Fig. 7.3 is shown in Fig. 7.4.
 Having drawn our grid then next thing to do is to use it to display a simple graph. This is done in Fig. 7.5.

Fig. 7.4 *Screen after running program in Fig. 7.3*

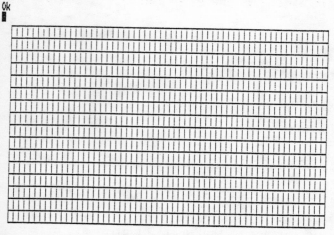

Fig 7.5

```
10 CLS
30 SCREEN 2
40 LINE(19,19)-(619,179),,B
50 FOR COL = 29 TO 609 STEP 10
60 LINE(COL,19)-(COL,179)
70 NEXT COL
80 FOR ROW = 29 TO 169 STEP 10
90 LINE(19,ROW)-(619,ROW)
100 NEXT ROW
110 FOR X=19 TO 599 STEP 10
120 LINE(X,179-((X)^2)/3000)-(X+19,179-((X+19)^2)/3000)
130 NEXT X
140 LOCATE 24,40:PRINT"X - axis"
150 LOCATE 12,1:PRINT"Y"
160 LOCATE 1,30:PRINT "Plotting a graph"
```

**Program outline: The first part of this program is the same
as the program in Fig.7.3. The graph that is plotted is that
of Y = X² and the because of the way that the pixels are
identified it has to be "scaled". First of all the steps on X
are in steps of ten pixels starting at 19, the left-hand edge
of the grid. This produces a value of Y that increases as
X gets bigger. But the pixel numbering system is such that
we want them to decrease as we proceed from the bottom
to the top, so Y has to be scaled by dividing the result of
the calculation by 3000 as well by taking the calculated
value of Y from 179. This places the point to be plotted
within the range of the grids. The LOCATE commands
move the text cursor to a specified row and column so that
a message or a heading can be placed at that point.**

When this program has been run the screen looks as shown
in Fig. 7.6.

Fig 7.6 *Screen after running the program in Fig. 7.5*

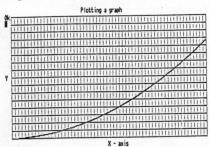

7.3 CIRCLES

Circles and ellipses, or parts of them, can be drawn using the **CIRCLE** command. This command consists of the word **CIRCLE** followed by a number of modifiers that define such things as the position of the centre of the circle, its radius and the start and end of the "sweep" that draws it. The program in Fig. 7.7 illustrates this and the result as displayed on the screen is shown in Fig. 7.8

Fig. 7.7

```
10 CLS
20 SCREEN 2
30 LINE(19,19)-(19,179)
40 LINE-(619,179)
50 LINE-(619,19)
60 LINE -(19,19)
65 FOR RADIUS = 0 TO 100 STEP 10
70 CIRCLE (319,99),RADIUS
80 NEXT RADIUS
```

Program outline: This program draws a box as before and then proceeds to draw a series of circles based on a centre at (319,99) which is the centre of the box, with ever increasing radii by the loop in lines 65 to 80.

Fig 7.8 *Screen after running program in Fig. 7.7*

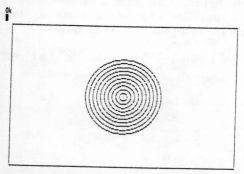

The next example, in Fig.7.9 shows how only part of a circle is drawn. It is similar to Fig. 7.7 but the **CIRCLE** command is followed by qualifiers to define the part of the circle that is to be drawn. Again the screen display is shown in the following illustration, Fig. 7.10.

Fig. 7.9

```
10 CLS
20 SCREEN 2
30 LINE(19,19)-(19,179)
40 LINE-(619,179)
50 LINE-(619,19)
60 LINE -(19,19)
65 FOR RADIUS = 0 TO 100 STEP 10
70 CIRCLE (319,99),RADIUS,,0,3.141593
80 NEXT RADIUS
```

Program outline: The important line is line 70. What follows the two commas after the radius specifier (this is because the qualifier that defines the colour of the circle has been omitted) give the start and finish angle of the "sweep". The starting angle is zero, measurements of angles in this context are always anti-clockwise from the horizontal, and the finishing angle is our old friend "pi". This is because the angles are measured in radians not degrees and 3.141593 radians is 180 degrees. Thus only the top half of the circles are drawn.

Fig 7.10 *Screen after running program in Fig. 7.9*

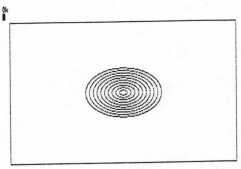

```
1LIST  2RUN▶  3LOAD" 4SAUE" 5CONT▶ 6,"LPT1 7TRON▶ 8TROFF▶ 9KEY  0SCREEN
```

To draw an ellipse the **CIRCLE** command has to be further modified by an "aspect" number. Because the screen of your PC is wider than it is high (notice there are more horizontal pixels than vertical pixels) the software does a conversion automatically when drawing a circle to take this into account. However, if you want to draw a series of ellipses in the same way as you drew the circles then the program in Fig. 7.11 will do this. The screen display is shown in Fig. 7.12.

Fig 7.11

```
10 CLS
20 SCREEN 2
30 LINE(19,19)-(19,179)
40 LINE-(619,179)
50 LINE-(619,19)
60 LINE -(19,19)
65 FOR RADIUS = 0 TO 100 STEP 10
70 CIRCLE (319,99),RADIUS,,,,5/18
80 NEXT RADIUS
```

Program outline: This is the same as the programs in Figs 7.9 and 7.10 except that there is another modifier on the end of the CIRCLE command. By varying this number you are telling the program that an ellipse is to be drawn. By default the number is 5/6 in medium resolution and 5/12 in high resolution and circles will be drawn. This "pulls" the ellipse that would be drawn into a circle. Change that figure to anything else and the "pulling" is not so great and an ellipse results.

Fig 7.12 *Screen after running program in Fig. 7.11*

1LIST   2RUN►   3LOAD"   4SAVE"   5CONT►   6,"LPT1   7TRON►   8TROFF►   9KEY   0SCREEN

7.4 PAINTING

To fill in parts of your graphics screen the **PAINT** command is used. A **PAINT** command requires at least a pair of coordinates as an argument. If the coordinates lie within a figure you have drawn then the figure is filled with colour. If they are outside the figure then the outside is filled with colour. The colour is defined by a modifier that immediately follows the coordinates and will be in the range 0 to 3. These two modifiers can be followed by two more that will define the border colour and the background colour.

PAINT(199,99),2,1

will start painting from the point with coordinates (199,99) and will paint the area filled with colour 2 and the border will be in colour 1.

Fig. 7.13 shows the screen after running a program that contains a **PAINT** command. There are several things to notice about it. One is that it sets the screen to medium resolution graphics which is why the characters are much bigger than usual. This is because the screen is only 40 characters wide. The other is that a list of the program has been asked for and it appears in the top left-hand corner of the screen. In the black-and-white of the illustration the circle appears as slightly greyer than the background. In fact the circle was white and the background was an orange/red colour. The command in line 30 deals with the colouring of the circle by defining the colour inside the circle (the coordinates specified by **PAINT** fall inside the circle) and the colour of the border of the circle. The rest of the screen (the coordinates of **PAINT** lie outside the circle, line 50) is then filled with the other colour.

Fig 7.13 *Program to paint colours inside drawn shape*

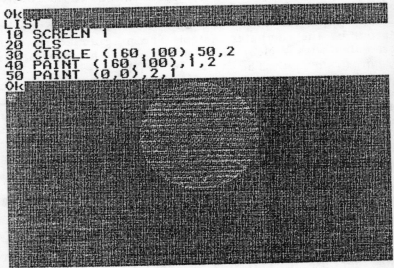

PUTTING PROGRAMMING TO WORK

8.1 INTRODUCTION

This chapter is largely about the birth, and its pangs, of a computer program written in BASIC. It has been said that programming is essentially a creative process and in some cases is akin to an art form. The latter statement is debatable, but the former is certainly true. A program usually starts with an idea, often in the form of a problem to be solved. In the case of professional programming it could be the result of the analysis of a system, say an invoicing or stock control system, and the production of a program specification. Such a specification would consist of a clear description of the type of data to be input into the program for processing and the information to be output by the computer system. The programmer is thus presented with a clear indication of what his program is *required to do*. The task is fairly clear cut and straightforward. After the programmer has written and tested the program it is handed over to other people to use. In fact much programming work is often simply a matter of *coding* into the appropriate computer language and as we shall see in later chapters the choice of language depends on the type of system being developed. Once the program design has been decided on the task of programming is comparatively simple.

Now that there is an ever-increasing number of PCs being used in smaller and smaller organisations the task of systems analyst, programmer and operator are tending to be merged into one. It is now quite common for a single person to specify the requirements of the program, write it and then use it. This is why there is an ever-growing requirement for people who are technically expert in some field who additionally need to learn and practise the skills of computer programming.

8.2 GETTING STARTED

The example to be used in this section is in itself quite trivial, but an attempt has been made to be as general as possible so that readers from all specialisms can relate to the ideas involved. The starting point is that of designing a simple computer game in which the computer chooses a number and the human player attempts to guess it. Initially the form of the program can be drawn in the form of an *outline flowchart* as shown in Fig. 8.1. The "clouds" in a flowchart represent operations which have to take place, but with no specific steps detailed in these clouds. The details begin to emerge in the first detailed flowchart, Fig. 8.2, where the shapes of the boxes follow a convention, which indicates the *kind of operation* taking place at this point. The most common are these

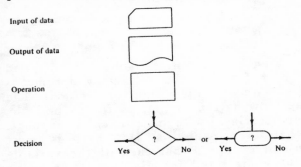

Input of data

Output of data

Operation

Decision

Fig 8.1 *Outline flowchart of operations*

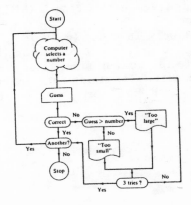

Fig 8.2 *Detailed flowchart of operation using flowchart symbols*

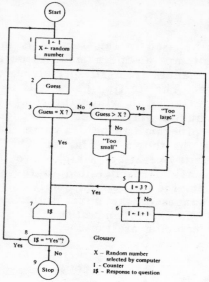

There are two things to be noticed about the detailed flowcharts. One is that we use the <-- sign, which means "takes the value of". We keep the = sign for *decisions*. The other is that the flowchart does not, as far as possible, contain statements associated with any particular language. The *glossary* that accompanies a flowchart is most important because it explains what each of the variable names used in the chart stand for. Having drawn out a flowchart and tested it by following specimen data through it - a so-called *dry run* - the next job is to convert it into some suitable language, in this case BASIC. If we number the boxes it becomes very easy to convert these into program line numbers. In order to avoid too many GOTO statements it is good practice to make the NO exit from a decision box go to the next number in sequence. It is even better, of course, if GOTO statements are not used at all. Fig. 8.3 shows a BASIC program written from the flowchart.

Fig 8.3

```
1 RANDOMIZE TIMER
10 I=1
11 X=INT(RND(0)*10)+1
20 INPUT G
30 IF G=X THEN 70
40 IF G>X THEN PRINT"Too large" ELSE PRINT"Too small"
50 IF I=3 THEN 70
60 I=I+1
65 GOTO 20
70 INPUT I$
80 IF I$="YES" THEN 1
90 STOP
```

You should note that GWBASIC requires that you use the command in line 1 if you want to ensure that a different set of random numbers are generated each time the program is run. **RND(0)** generates a random number in the range 0 to 1.

8.3 CREATING ANOTHER PROGRAM

This problem involves the merging of two sorted lists again, but the approach this time is not through the medium of a flowchart but uses the "top down" approach. This leads to a structured program. First of all we have to read the two lists into RAM. Then we have to merge them in such a way that we compare pairs of numbers from each list and allocate the appropriate one to the merged list. Finally we print out the two original lists and the new merged list. At this point we at least know what our objectives are and so we could write them down in the following way:

(1)   Read the two lists into memory
(2)   Loop while there are numbers left in each list
(3)   Allocate the next number in turn from each list according to its size into the new list
(4)   Display the original lists and the new merged list

These steps have now to be expanded to give us more detail, since we now should have realised that we have continually to compare pairs of numbers, one from each list, and place the smaller of the two in the new list. Then we have to pick up the next number from the list which provided the smaller number and perform another comparison. This we continue until we have used up all the numbers from one list. Then we write the remaining numbers from the other list into the new, merged, list. To start the program off we have to compare the pair of numbers taken from the head of each list. Then we have to pick up the next number from the list which provided the one just written out to the new list. Here is an **IF . . THEN . . . ELSE** type of situation. There is also a hint of two subroutines; one to collect the next item from one of the two lists and the other to write a number into the new list, which is what we did with the version of the problem in Fig. 6.5.

If we call the original lists **A** and **B** and the new merged list **C** we can write the program in more detail

```
1. Read the lists A and B into memory
2. Set the first number in List A to the variable P
3. Set the first number in List B to the variable Q
4. Loop
5.          If P<Q
6.                  Then
7.                              Place P into List C
8.                              Get next number from List A
9.                              Set this number to the variable P
10.                 Else
11.                             Place Q into List C
12.                             Get next number from List B
13.                             Set this number to the variable Q
14.         Ifend
15.Repeat until one of the lists is exhausted
16.Place rest of the remaining list into List C
17.Print List A
18.Print List B
19.Print List C
```

Notice that we have written our program with no **GOTO** statements. The loop has been defined by the statements in lines 4 and 15 and all the instruction contained within these are executed as required by the decision in line 5.

The program outline lends itself very well to the insertion of subroutines and we can now identify four of these. They are a subroutine to read a list into memory, another to print it out, one to get the next number from one of the lists and allocate it either to **P** or **Q** as appropriate, and finally a subroutine to add either **P** or **Q** to the list **C**. We will look at these subroutines in turn. First of all, **LISTREAD**.

```
SUBROUTINE LISTREAD (NO,L)
1. Read NO
2. For counter = 1 to NO
3.        Read item
4.        Set L(counter):=item
```

```
5. Repeat
RETURN TO MAIN PROGRAM
```

In the main program we will write

```
CALL LISTREAD(N1,A)
```

if we want to read a set of numbers into the list **A**, **N1** will hold the number of numbers in the list.

Similarly a subroutine called **LISTPRINT** will print out the contents of a specified list

```
SUBROUTINE LISTPRINT(N,L)
1. For counter = 1 to N
2.      Print L(counter)
3. Repeat
RETURN TO MAIN PROGRAM
```

We have already seen the subroutines **GETNEXT** and **ADD** forming part of an earlier version of this program, so let us write them down in a structured way

```
SUBROUTINE GETNEXT(H,X,M,E,N)
1. Set E:=0
2. If M>N
3.      Then            Set E:=1
4.
5.      Else
6.                      Set H:=X(M)
7.                      Set M:=M+1
8. Ifend
RETURN TO MAIN PROGRAM
```

E is the variable which tells us whether we have reached the end of the list named **X**.

ADD looks like this

```
SUBROUTINE ADD (H,C,K)
1. Set C(K):=H
2. Set K:=K+1
RETURN TO MAIN PROGRAM
```

So now we can construct our complete program in the following way

```
1. CALL LISTREAD(N1,A)
2. CALL LISTREAD(N2,B)
3. Set P:=A(1)          **P set to 1st number in A**
4. Set Q:=B(1)          **Q set to 1st number in B**
5. Set L:= 2            **L points to next number in A**
6. Set K:= 1            **K points to next number in C**
7. Set J:=2             **J points to next number in B**
```

```
8. Loop
9.          If P<Q
10.                 Then
11.                             CALL ADD(P,C,K)
12.                             CALL GETNEXT(P,A,L,E,N1)
13.                 Else
14.                             CALL ADD(Q,C,K)
15.                             CALL GETNEXT(Q,,B,J,E,N2)
16.          Ifend
17. Repeat until E=1
18. Loop
19.          If P<Q               **This decides which list is exhausted**
20.                 Then
21.                             CALL ADD(Q,,C,K)
22.                             CALL GETNEXT(Q,B,J,E,N2)
23.                 Else
24.                             CALL ADD(P,C,K)
25.                             CALL GETNEXT(P,A,L,E,N1)
26.          Ifend
27. Repeat until E=1
28. CALL LISTPRINT(N1,A)
29. CALL LISTPRINT(N2,B)
30. Set N:=N1+N2
31. CALL LISTPRINT(N,C)
```

To illustrate this program in action we are going to code it in the version of BASIC used by the Open University. This is a structured version of the language, as distinct from the more common versions of BASIC. It also allows us to use such things as **REPEAT . . . UNTIL**. The subroutines are defined at the end of the program and will be called **READ**, **ADD**, **GET** and **PRINT**. Notice how the lists are referred to in the subroutine calls and the parameter lists for the subroutines themselves by having the name followed by an empty pair of brackets. The program is listed in Fig. 8.4 and the listing is followed by a demonstration run of the program.

Fig 8.4

```
10 DIM A(100),B(100),C(100),X(100)
20 PRINT "FIRST LIST :-;
30 CALL READ(N1,A())
40 PRINT "SECOND LIST :-";
50 CALL READ(N2,B())
60 PRINT
70 P=A(1)
80 Q=B(1)
90 L=2
100 K=1
110 J=2
  0 REPEAT
        IF P<Q THEN
```

```
140     CALL ADD(P,C,(),K)
150     CALL GET(P,A(),L,E,N1)
160   ELSE
170     CALL ADD(Q,C(),K)
180     CALL GET(Q,B(),J,E,N2)
190   EIF
200 UNTIL E=1
210 REPEAT
220   IF P>Q THEN
230     CALL ADD(Q,C(),K)
240     CALL GET(Q,B(),J,E,N2)
250   ELSE
260     CALL ADD(P,C(),K)
270     CALL GET(P,A(),L,E,N1)
280   EIF
290 UNTIL E=1
300 PRINT
310 PRINT "FIRST LIST"
320 PRINT "=========="
330 CALL PRINT(N1,A())
340 PRINT
350 PRINT
360 PRINT "SECOND LIST"
370 PRINT "==========="
380 CALL PRINT(N2,B())
390 N=N1+N2
400 PRINT
410 PRINT
420 PRINT "MERGED LIST"
430 PRINT "==========="
440 CALL PRINT(N,C())
450 END


460 SUB READ(NO,L())
470 PRINT "HOW MANY NUMBERS ";
480 INPUT NO
490 FOR C=1 TO NO
500     INPUT L(C)
510 NEXT C
520 END


530 SUB ADD(H,C(),K)
540 C(K)=H
550 K=K+1
560 END


570 SUB GET(H,X(),M,E,N)
580 E=0
590 IF M>N THEN
600   E=1
610 ELSE
620   H=X(M)
```

102

```
630    M=M+1
640 EIF
650 END


660 SUB PRINT(N,L())
670 FOR C=1 TO N
680    PRINT L(C);
690 NEXT C
700 END

RUN

FIRST LIST :- HOW MANY NUMBERS?12
?3
?5
?6
?8
?9
?14
?16
?18
?19
?20
?26
?28
SECOND LIST :- HOW MANY NUMBERS?10
?1
?2
?7
?11
?17
?30
?32
?45
?50
?55
```

FIRST LIST
==========
```
 3   5   6   8   9   14   16   18   19   20
26  28
```

SECOND LIST
==========
```
 1   2   7   11   17   30   32   45   50   55
```

MERGED LIST
==========
```
1    2    3    5    6    7    8    9    11   14   16
17   18   19   20   26   28   30   32   45   50   55
```

DONE

8.4 FILLING IN THE DETAILS

By the time we have reached this stage we should have a program that works. In our case we may not have a very exciting program, but at least it does work. However it has been designed to run in an *interactive* mode. This means that it runs in *real time* and the user is in constant communication with the computer system. BASIC is not the only computer language that enables you to, as it were, "hold a conversation with the computer". As you will see later on in this book other computer languages can produce programs that can be used in a similar manner. BASIC is used for all the current examples because it is easy to learn and programs written in this language are very easy to edit and amend. The program so far looks a little "cold" to a user who is not familiar with the program. A simple "?" with no indication of what is expected in the way of a response is not very "user-friendly" and is certainly no way to inspire confidence or sympathy with computer systems as a whole. The addition of a few **PRINT** statements makes the program more attractive. The flowchart now amended is shown in Fig. 8.5 with the corresponding program and a run in Fig. 8.6.

The game can now be developed into one which is more sophisticated. In this a four-digit number is generated by the computer and the human player is asked what it is. This time the computer tells the contestant if he has made any correct guesses (bulls) of digits in their correct places in the number, or a correct digit chosen but in the wrong place in the number (cows). An outline flowchart for this is shown in Fig. 8.7.

Fig. 8.8 is an expansion of section A in the flowchart in Fig. 8.7. The three part box is a good way of showing a loop in a flowchart, in fact it uses a more "structured" approach to programming by hinting at a **FOR . . . NEXT** type of loop. The top left-hand corner of the box shows the string point of the loop with the initial value of the starting variable called **I**. The bottom left-hand box shows the amount by which **I** is to be incremented each time the loop is traversed. The right-hand side of the block is really saying "while" the index **I** is less than or equal to 4 the path from the bottom of the box is taken. When the test finally fails the right-hand exit is taken. In this part of the program the first digit of the guess is tested against the first digit of the computer-chosen number. Then the pair of second digits are compared. The score of "bulls" is kept in the variable **B**. You should note that the code N$(I,I) is used to stand for the Ith character in the string N$. This is because it is not a good idea to write down statements that could be construed to be something in the BASIC language.

Fig. 8.5 *The amended flowchart*

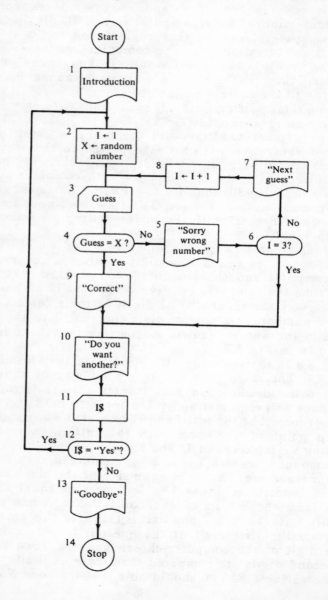

Fig 8.6

```
1 RANDOMIZE TIMER
5 PRINT"I shall choose a number between 1 and 10. You have
three guesses"
10 I=1
11 X=INT(RND(0)*10)+1
20 INPUT G
30 IF G=X THEN PRINT"Correct": GOTO 70 ELSE PRINT "Sorry,
wrong number ";
40 IF G>X THEN PRINT"- too large" ELSE PRINT"- too small"
50 IF I=3 THEN 70
55 PRINT"Next guess"
60 I=I+1
65 GOTO 20
70 PRINT"Do you want another ";:INPUT I$
80 IF I$="YES" THEN 1
90 PRINT"GOODBYE":STOP
RUN
I shall choose a number between 1 and 10. You have three
guesses
? 3
Sorry, wrong number - too large
Next guess
? 5
Sorry, wrong number - too large
Next guess
? 2
Sorry, wrong number - too large
Do you want another
? YES
I shall choose a number between 1 and 10. You have three
guesses
? 1
Sorry, wrong number - too small
Next guess
? 3
Correct
Do you want another
? YES
I shall choose a number between 1 and 10. You have three
guesses
? 4
Correct
Do you want another
? No
GOODBYE
```

Fig 8.7 *Outline flowchart for bulls and cows game*

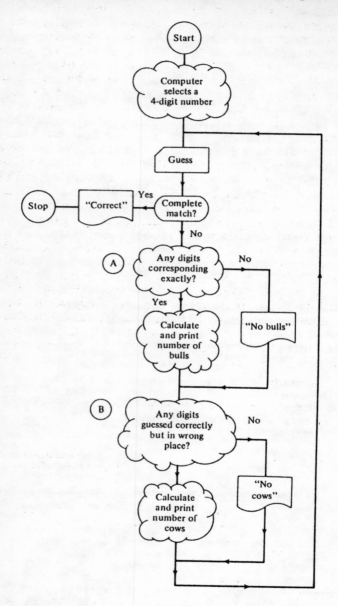

Fig. 8.9 is an attempt to expand section B in the flowchart in Fig. 8.7. At first sight the loop within a loop looks quite satisfactory for finding if any digits in the guess, **G$**, exist anywhere in the string of four digits called **N$**. But what if there are two occurrences of, say, the digit 4 in **N$** and only one in **G$**? In order to overcome this problem the two program segments need to be amended by the introduction of a new string variable called **Z$**. At the start of section A, **Z$** is set to contain the characters "****" and if identical digits occur in both **G$** and **N$** then **Z$** has that digit placed in the appropriate position. For example, if **G$** is "4376" and **N$** is "4697" then at the exit from the segment **Z$** becomes "4***" and **B** has the value of 1. Fig. 8.10 shows the amended version. In Fig. 8.11 the other segment is shown in its new form so that use is made of the newly introduced **Z$**. Finally a complete flowchart, Fig. 8.12, can be put together. The BASIC program derived from the final flowchart is shown in Fig. 8.13.

Although at this stage the task of writing the program could be thought of as being complete, this is true only so long as it is left running under the particular version of BASIC it was designed for. If, on the other hand, it is intended to make it possible for the program to be run under as many versions of the language as possible, then a few notes about any variations would be helpful. Also, the original author may not be around when someone wants to start making changes to the program. A set of useful notes is shown in Fig. 8.14.

Fig 8.8 *Expansion of section A of flowchart in Fig. 8.7*

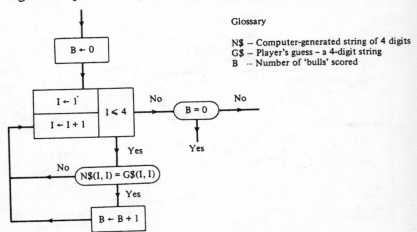

Glossary

N$ – Computer-generated string of 4 digits
G$ – Player's guess – a 4-digit string
B -- Number of 'bulls' scored

Fig 8.9 *Attempt to expand section B of flowchart in Fig. 8.7*

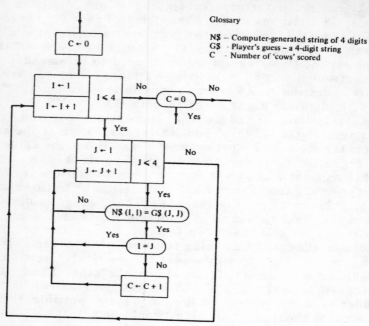

Glossary

N$ – Computer-generated string of 4 digits
G$ – Player's guess – a 4-digit string
C – Number of 'cows' scored

Fig 8.10 *Amended version of Fig. 8.9*

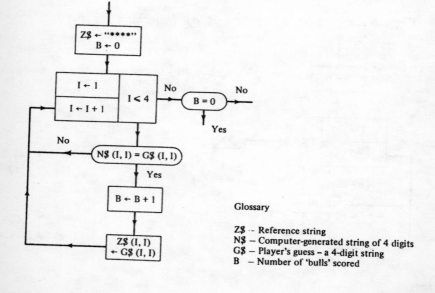

Glossary

Z$ – Reference string
N$ – Computer-generated string of 4 digits
G$ – Player's guess – a 4-digit string
B – Number of 'bulls' scored

Fig 8.11 *Introducing* **Z$**

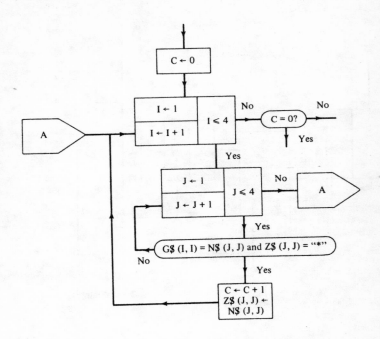

Glossary

Z$ — Reference string
N$ — Computer-generated string of 4 digits
G$ — Player's guess – a 4-digit string
C — Number of 'cows' scored

110

Fig. 8.12 *The complete flowchart*

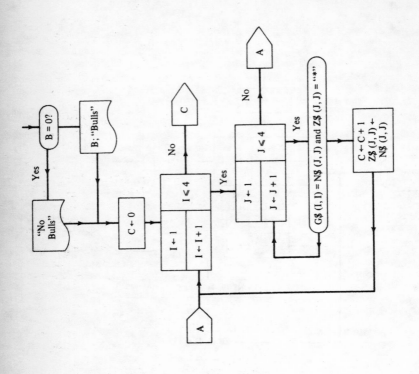

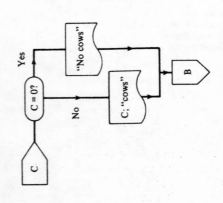

Glossary

A$ — String of digits > 1 to 9
N$ — Computer-generated 4-digit string
G$ — Player's guess — 4-digit string
Z$ — Reference string
I, J, K — Indexes to individual characters in string
B — Number of 'bulls'
C — Number of 'cows'

111

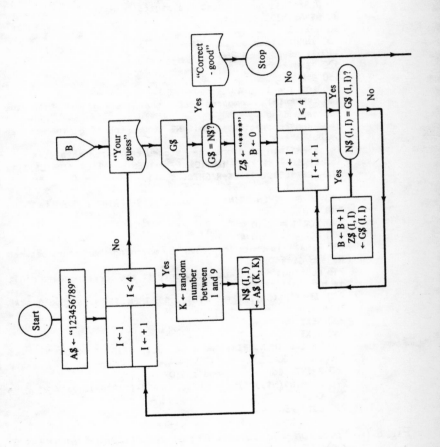

Fig 8.11

Fig 8.13

```
10 A$="123456789"
20 N$=""
30 RANDOMIZE TIMER
35 REM**This loop places four digits in string N$**
40 FOR I= 1 TO 4
50 K=INT(RND(0)*8)+1
60 RANDOMIZE TIMER
70 REM**This accumulates the digits in N$**
80 N$=N$+MID$(A$,K,1)
90 NEXT I
100 INPUT "Your guess ";G$
110 IF G$=N$ THEN 260
120 Z$="****"
130 B=0
140 FOR I = 1 TO 4
145 REM**This compares each character of G$ with the corresponding
146 REM**characters** of N$ thus counting the number of"bulls"**
147 REM**Then it drops the matched character into Z$**
150 IF MID$(N$,I,1)=MID$(G$,I,1) THEN B=B+1:C$=MID$(G$,I,1):Z$=LEFT$(Z$,I-1)+C$+RIGHT$(Z$,4-I)
160 NEXT I
170 IF B=0 THEN PRINT "No bulls" ELSE PRINT B;" Bulls"
180 C=0
190 FOR I = 1 TO 4
200 FOR J = 1 TO 4
215 REM**This looks for "cows" by matching characters between N$ and G$**
216 REM**and notches up a cow only if the corresponding digit is not in Z$**
210 IF MID$(G$,I,1)=MID$(N$,J,1) THEN IF MID$(Z$,J,1)="*" THEN 270
220 NEXT J
230 NEXT I
240 IF C=0 THEN PRINT "No cows" ELSE PRINT C;" Cows"
250 GOTO 100
260 PRINT "Correct - Good": STOP
270 C$=MID$(N$,J,1):Z$=LEFT$(Z$,J-1)+C$+RIGHT$(Z$,4-J)
280 C=C+1
290 GOTO 230
```

Fig 8.14 *Notes on the variations of BASIC used in the BANDC program*

(1)   Use of the word RANDOMIZE may vary from version to version. Lines 30 and 60.

(2)   RND(0) may have to be replaced by RND(X), RND(-1) or RND(1). Line 50.

(3)   You cannot use MID$(N$,I,1) on the left-hand side of an = sign, so you have to accumulate the

string of digits in a special way. Lines 80, 150 and 270.

(4) Some versions of BASIC use ., instead of ;. Line 100.

(5) Not every version of BASIC allows you to have instructions on the same line separated by : characters. Line 150, 270.

(6) You can use AND instead of THEN in some versions. Line 210.

If you insert an extra line, line 95,

    95 PRINT N$

before you run the program you will get a result similar to that shown in Fig. 8.15.

Fig. 8.15

```
Ok
LOAD"bandc
Ok
95 ?n$
RUN
5481
Your guess ? 4592
No bulls
  2  Cows
Your guess ? 5492
  2  Bulls
No cows
Your guess ? 5814
  1  Bulls
  3  Cows
Your guess ? 5418
  2  Bulls
  2  Cows
Your guess ? 5481
Correct - Good
Break in 260
Ok
```

1LIST   2RUN←   3LOAD" 4SAVE" 5CONT← 6,"LPT1 7TRON← 8TROFF← 9KEY   0SCREEN

The notes on a program are part of the documentation associated with it and should be kept for reference together with other details about the program such as

(1) Program name
(2) Author
(3) Date written
(4) Specification of program requirements
(5) General description of the program and its operation
(6) Flowcharts or any other recognised program structure charts

(7)   Input/output requirements

(8)   Tape or disk file and record formats

(9)   Specification of storage and the use of peripherals

(10)   Coding sheets and/or program listings

(11)   Data preparation requirements and operating instructions

(12)   Program development documentation

(13)   Any modifications made to the program during its life

Fig. 8.16 shows a sample of the kind of information given about the bulls and cows program.

It is often useful to include, for quick reference, remarks or comments within the the program itself. All high-level languages provide the facility to do this.

Fig 8.16

PROGRAM: BANDC (Game of Bulls and Cows)
WRITTEN BY P.E.GOSLING
DATE: 21st January 1981
Version 2 written 6th February 1989
Written for IBM PCs and compatible machines running on MS-DOS or PC-DOS versions 2 and above and in Microsoft GWBASIC Version 3.3.

8.5 SOME VARIATIONS

The next two examples show how you can go a long way towards making simpler BASIC programs by getting rid of **GOTO** statements by using **IF . . . THEN . . . ELSE . . .** statements.The first of these is the electricity bill program, which will turn up again. Fig. 8.17 is the program written from the simple flowchart in Fig. 1.1 (p.5).

Fig 8.17

```
10 INPUT E
20 IF E<= 150 THEN 40
30 GOTO 120
40 C=E*.07
45 PRINT C
50 IF C<3.64 THEN 70
60 GOTO 80
70 C=3.64
80 C=C+3.25
85 PRINT C
90 C=C*1.15
100 PRINT C
```

```
110 END
120 E=E-150
130 C=E*.05+10.5
140 GOTO 80
150 END
```

Fig. 8.18 shows the same program written using the more structured outline shown also on p. 5.

Fig 8.18

```
10 INPUT UNITS
20 IF UNITS<=150 THEN COST=UNITS*.07 ELSE
COST=10.5+(UNITS-150)*.05
30 IF COST<3.64 THEN COST = 3.64
40 COST = (COST+3.25)*1.15
50 PRINT COST
```

The second example is a program to convert from one currency to another. Fig. 8.19 shows the program written using **GOTO**s.

Fig 8.19

```
20 INPUT "Currency: ",C$
30 PRINT "How many ";C$; " ";
40 INPUT "to the pound:";P
50 INPUT "Convert 'To' or 'From' sterling ";S$
60 IF S$="To" THEN 200
70 INPUT "How many pounds";N
80 S=N*P
90 PRINT N;"Pounds = ";S;C$
100 STOP
200 PRINT "How many ";C$;" ";
210 INPUT N
220 S=N/P
230 PRINT N;C$;"=";S;"pounds"
240 STOP
```

Fig. 8.20 shows the same program as written using the **IF ... THEN ... ELSE ...** instructions.

Fig 8.20

```
20 INPUT "Currency: ",C$
30 PRINT "How many ";C$; " ";
40 INPUT "to the pound:";P
50 INPUT "Convert 'To' or 'From' sterling ";S$
60 IF S$="To" THEN PRINT "How many ";C$;" ";:INPUT
N:S=N/P:PRINT N;C$;"=";S;"Pounds" ELSE INPUT "How many
pounds";N:S=N*P:PRINT N;"Pounds = ";S;C$
70 END
```

CHAPTER 9

BUG HUNTING

OR WHY MY PROGRAM

NEVER WORKS FIRST TIME

9.1 INTRODUCTION

This chapter applies particularly to debugging programs written in BASIC, but the general ideas are applicable to programs written in all computer languages.

It is almost a law of Nature that no program of more than four lines ever works first time. The reasons for this are manifold but they can usually be put down in many cases to very simple errors of typing or the use of the computer language itself. Errors in computer programs are called *bugs* and the various ways of *debugging* a program form the basis of this chapter. An attempt is made to itemise the various types of errors but it is often a combination of several of these which cause a program to fail.

9.2 TYPING ERRORS

This type of error is sometimes difficult to spot since it is a human failing to see only what we want to see, particularly when checking a program listing. We strike the wrong key and produce an error which fools both us and BASIC. For example, one program the author wrote consistently failed to work properly and eventually the error was tracked down to a line which should have read

        215 LET T = 10

having been mistyped as

        215 LEY T = 10

Now it is true to say that LEY is not a BASIC instruction but the BASIC interpreter being used at that time allowed variable names to be longer than one letter - GWBASIC is a case in point. Not only that but the **LET**, as is common nowadays, was optional and so a variable called **LEY T** was allotted the value 10, because that version allowed spaces in names. This of course is a good argument for not using **LET**. The moral is that you should always check a program very carefully.

9.3 WRONGLY LABELLED INSTRUCTIONS

An error caused by wrongly labelled instructions, line numbers in the case of BASIC, is often difficult to find. This is because the fault is shown up by an error message which says that a jump cannot be made to a label that does not exist. The problem then becomes one of finding where the jump ought to have been made in the first place. If it is not possible, then a good way to detect this type of error is to issue the **RENUMBER** command. This will attempt to renumber the lines of the program and any unresolved **GOTO**s will be produce a message such as

Undefined line number in xxx

In this case the detective work has to start to find where the jump should have been made to in the first place. Once this inconsistency has been sorted out the program can be run again. This is, of course, a very good argument for having programs with as few **GOTO**s as possible.

9.4 WRONGLY NESTED LOOPS

If one loop lies within another then it must lie wholly within it. A program may have a section such as

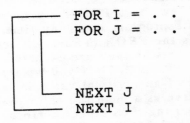

```
FOR I = . .
  FOR J = . .


  NEXT J
NEXT I
```

which is fine. But to have an arrangement such as

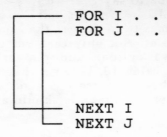

```
    FOR I . .
    FOR J . .



    NEXT I
    NEXT J
```

is illegal and will cause messages such as

NEXT WITHOUT FOR

or

FOR WITHOUT NEXT

to be displayed.

9.5 HARD LOOPS

At its worst this error is typifies by a program statement such as

45 GOTO 45

This error is usually observed when there is apparently nothing happening when some form of display is expected. If this is observed then it is best to stop execution (press the **Ctrl** and **Break** keys simultaneously is usually the best for BASIC programs) and then the program will halt and the line number where it has stopped will be displayed. Key in **CONT** and execution can be resumed if you wish. If you are in doubt about the path of the program then insert a few extra **PRINT** statements which will indicate where the program is at any time. Another facility with BASIC is the **TRON** (**TR**ace **ON**) command. This lists the line numbers as they are executed. This is turned off by **TROFF** (**TR**ace **OFF**). If you wish you can get a display of the state of any critical variable as the program proceeds. These serve as a good indicator that all is, or is not, well. Remember that PCs do not perform some calculations very quickly, and what appears to be a hard loop is in fact a perfectly correct, but lengthy, set of calculations.

9.6 PROBLEMS WITH LOOPS

This type of error can be very frustrating to search for and is due to the fact that not all loops work in the same way. The simple program shown below illustrates the point. Try it on your PC and see the result.

```
10 INPUT A,B,C
20 FOR I = A TO B STEP C
30 PRINT I;
40 NEXT I
50 PRINT "EXIT VALUE OF I";I
60 END
```

Use values of **A**, **B** and **C** of 1,10,1 then 1,1,1 and finally 5,1,1 and compare the outputs with those shown in Fig. 9.1. This shows the results of running the program under different versions of BASIC. The differences occur because of the different points in the loop where the index variable, **I**, is updated. Also note that it is possible to traverse a loop even though the target value is smaller than the initial value of **I** with a positive step size.

Another problem you may come across is with **WHILE . . . WEND** loops. If you are not careful you may find that you put yourself in a position where you will never go through the loop at all. This program is a case in point

```
10 WHILE X<>0
15 INPUT X
20 T=T+X
30 WEND
40 PRINT T
```

This is a simple loop to add up a series of numbers using an input value of zero for a trigger. Because the instructions say "perform the loop instructions while **X** has a value of zero" it will never even enter the loop because although a value of **X** has not been specified BASIC assumes that it is zero. Hence **X** has a value that fails the test at once, that is it is **NOT** not equal to zero.

A good general rule when dealing with loops is always to set the counter *before* going into the loop and increment *within the loop*. Then use a ">" condition at the end rather than a "=" to ensure that the condition is matched.

120

Fig 9.1

Program run on system 1

```
10 INPUT A,B,C
20 FOR I = A TO B STEP C
30     PRINT I;
40 NEXT I
50 PRINT "EXIT VALUE OF I ";I
60 END
RUN

?1,10,1
1  2  3  4  5  6  7  8  9  10  9  10                                    EXIT VALUE
OF I 11

DONE
RUN
?1,1,1
1    EXIT VALUE OF I 2

DONE
RUN
?5,1,1
EXIT VALUE OF I 5
```

Program run on system 2

```
10 INPUT A,B,C
20 FOR I = A TO B STEP C
30 PRINT I;
40 NEXT I
50 PRINT "EXIT VALUE OF I ";I
60 END
RUN
? 1,10,1
1  2  3  4  5  6  7  8  9  10 EXIT VALUE OF I 11

READY
?1,1,1
1 EXIT VALUE OF I 2

READY
?5,1,1
5 EXIT VALUE OF I 6

READY
```

Program run on system 3

```
10 INPUT A,B,C
*20 FOR I = A TO B STEP C
*30 PRINT I;
*40 NEXT I
```

```
*50 PRINT "EXIT VALUE OF I ";I
*60 END
*RUN
?1,10,1
1  2  3  4  5  6  7  8  9  10 EXIT VALUE OF I  10

END AT 0060
*RUN
?1,1,1
1 EXIT VALUE OF I 1

END AT 0060
*RUN
?5,1,1
EXIT VALUE OF I 5
END AT 0060
```

9.7 INTERPRETER ERRORS

These are errors discovered by BASIC on an attempt to run
a program when using a PC. As has already been
mentioned, when a program is typed in line by line the
lines are placed in RAM and they are not interpreted until
the **RUN** command is issued. When BASIC finds an error
the program halts and only when the error has been
corrected will BASIC be able to get past the line with the
error. Unless a command such as

> RUN 70

can be issued - **RUN** from line 70 - **RUN** will always cause
execution to start from the lowest numbered line of the
program. It is therefore important to test each program
thoroughly by making sure that every possible jump is
made so that no incorrect lines are left lurking about in
the background ready to stop the program when an
unexpected piece of data is processed. The most common
errors will usually be identified by error messages such as

> UNMATCHED PARENTHESES

which refers to an unequal number of left- and right-hand
brackets,

> UNDEFINED VARIABLE

which refers to a variable whose value has not previously
been defined. GWBASIC tends to assign values of zero to
anything that has not been given a value,

OVERFLOW

where an attempt has been made to divide by zero,

SUBSCRIPT OUT OF BOUNDS

when an attempt has been made to use a value of a subscript larger than has been allowed for by a **DIM** statement.

FUNCTION ARGUMENT

applies, for example, when an attempt has been made to find the square root of a negative number.

The most common error issued by any computer language is

SYNTAX ERROR

which covers a multitude of sins and means that you attempted to use the language incorrectly. Typical errors of this type are embodied in a "program" such as

```
10 PRIMPT X
20 OUTPUT X
30 WHEN X=5 THEN 65
40 LET Y=X:P
50 LET P=3(X+Y)
6O END
```

In the last line of the above the letter **O** has been used instead of a zero. This is all right if you use a typewriter, but not a PC keyboard.

9.8 **CHOOSING TEST DATA**

Many programs contain errors which can be detected before it becomes too late by the use of suitable test data. If the program copes with the test data successfully then it can be said that it is safe to use for the purpose for which it is intended. For example, in Section 9.6 a program which tests how **FOR . . . NEXT** loops works is described. Three sets of test data were suggested for use at that point. These tested for an expected situation where the start value was less than the target value, a not so common situation where the start value and target values were equal and an unexpected situation where the target value was less than the initial value for a positive increment. If a program is written to sort a set of numbers, or names, into ascending order what better that a set of data arranged initially in descending order? By choosing good test data all parts of a program can be tested. There is nothing worse than having a program containing a section which has never been tested and thus - as has already been mentioned - containing a possible syntax error. This problem is overcome when we use compiled languages when the syntax is checked before we ever get the chance to run the program. But the choice of adequate test data against the possibility of run time errors is very important.

9.9 EXPECTING THE COMPUTER TO DO THE IMPOSSIBLE

There are times when the programmer can be carried away with the thrill of writing complicated programs. It is very easy to forget that a machine has only finite resources, such as a fixed amount of memory. An example of this is the program which contains

45 IF X%=10000000 THEN 200

forgetting that a signed integer (the % sign after the **X** defines it as an integer rather than a floating point number) on a PC has to be fitted into two bytes of memory; two bytes equals 16 bits, and can only store a number smaller than

$$2^{15} = 32768$$

allowing one bit for the sign.

A similar mistake is made in the program which contains

10 DIM A(200,400)

thus expecting an array to be stored containing 80 000 elements, and that on a machine with only 48K bytes of memory. Luckily most PCs these days have around 512K bytes of RAM and so this problem is not quite so pressing. However, because the more complex a program is the less RAM is left for data after the program has been loaded into memory. And do not forget that the memory has to store a large part of the operating system, MS-DOS or PC-DOS and the BASIC interpreter as well as your program before it starts doing anything else. In order to find out how much memory is available to you the command

    PRINT FRE(0)

will return the number of bytes available.

THE DBASE
PROGRAMMING LANGUAGE

10.1 INTRODUCTION

Ashton Tate gave birth to the dBase language in the mid 1970s with their first interpreter dBASE II. The product was improved product over the years with various updates and new versions dBASE III, dBASE III PLUS, and now their recently released dBASE IV, which according to the computer press is not as compatible as it might be. Whilst the popularity of dBASE has grown several other companies have produced other similar products with higher specifications, and enhancements to the language which also use the dBASE language syntax. These include:

Wordtech's pseudo compiler called dB Compiler
FoxSoftware's interpreter/compiler FoxBase
Nantucket's compiler called Clipper
MegaTechs's pseudo compiler dBFast.

Clipper is the only one that produces a true .EXE compiled program that does not require a run time module. The main advantages of this are speed of execution, no need for expensive interpreters like dBASE III PLUS itself, and no royalties payable on the compiled program. This demonstrates a considerable saving if, as in this case, several copies of the program are required.

The dBASE programming language is designed to be used in conjunction with data files created by the dBASE database management program. It is a powerful structured language that makes use of a number of the features we have come across in BASIC. There is a **WHILE** statement and an **IF . . . THEN . . . ELSE . . .** construction that we shall see at work in this chapter.

10.2 THE ELECTRICITY BILL PROGRAM

The first example to be demonstrated is a program in the dBASE programming language to perform the electricity bill calculation. Programs in this language can be entered via any word processor that produces ASCII text files or by the dBASE word processor that comes with the program. As you run one of these programs it detects errors and displays suitable error messages - which sometimes are rather confusing as they do not always specify what kind of error it is. If you create the program using the package's own word processor you enter by keying in the command

MODIFY COMMAND ELEC

where in this case **ELEC** is going to be the name of the program. You simply key in the program instructions line by line exactly as they appear on the screen as shown in Fig. 10.1

You should notice that the program looks very similar to a BASIC program using such words as **INPUT, IF . . . THEN . . . ELSE** and the ? character for a print command. The two commands at the start of the program are to eliminate "talk back" by the program in the first instance. A feature that can be very useful in dBASE is that every time arithmetic is performed the value of the answer is displayed and every time a dBASE command is entered in a program a response is displayed. This is useful when debugging a program but not otherwise. When a program is run every program statement is echoed on the screen and

Fig 10.1

```
SET TALK OFF
SET ECHO OFF
CLEAR
INPUT "How many units ?" TO units
IF units < 150
cost=units*0.07
ELSE
cost=10.5+(units-150)*.05
ENDIF
IF cost<3.64
THEN cost=3.64
ENDIF
cost=(cost+3.25)*1.15
? "Total cost of electricity:" ,cost
```

this too is eliminated by the **SET ECHO OFF** instruction. You will notice how closely this program follows the structured layout on p.5. **CLEAR** clears the screen before the program runs.

10.3 A TYPICAL dBASE PROGRAM

This next example is a program that utilises the particular features of this database programming language. It enables you to manipulate data that is stored, in this example, in two files. One of these is a stock list, shown truncated in this case, and the other is a catalogue file that is related to the stock list. The latter is called **CATALOG.DBF** and the former is called **STOCK.DBF**, the **.DBF** extension denoting database files.

The stock file contains the records shown in Fig. 10.2 and each record contains seven fields. They are, in order, the stock reference, the number of the item in each pack, the bin code, the cost price per pack, the date of the last delivery, the reorder level and the number currently in stock.

Fig. 10.3 shows the contents of the catalog file. The fields in this case are the stock reference and the description in words of what the stock item is.

The object of the program listed in Fig. 10.4 is to enable the user to enquire of the state of any one of the stock items. The program produces a screen display as shown in Fig. 10.5.

Fig 10.2

```
AA1001 ,10, P1 ,2.35,14/07/88,250,344
AA1002 ,20, G1 ,3.44,05/05/88,150,567
AA1003 ,25, S3 ,7.88,08/06/88,200,267
AA1005 ,50, A3 ,5.77,12/09/88,250,321
AB1002 ,10, J8 ,7.88,12/0488,300,520
AB1200 ,1, A3 ,16.88,14/04/88,500,601
AC1002 ,50, H7 ,16.66,12/03/88,100,101
AC1003 ,5, S ,7.88,13/02/88,500,750
AF3005 ,25, F6 ,10.77,27/07/88,125,1178
AG3006 ,1, S ,16.99,01/07/88,50,123
AH5009 ,12, P3 ,18.55,06/07./88,125,500
```

```
BA1002 ,20,  H4 ,5.66,12/09/88,300,555
BA2005 ,25,  K8 ,17.88,03/04/88,100,450
BC3450 ,10,  S2 ,23.77,11/07/88,150,167
BD4545 ,12,  T5 ,21.77,13/05/88,175,223
BE7878 ,50,  J7 ,24.55,07/08/88,200,501
BF2310 ,100, H3 ,45.88,01/07/88,125,210
BG1003 ,50,  S2 ,27.55,04/06/88,250,432
BH6754 ,10,  M4 ,20.00,17/03/88,100,317
BJ1004 ,25,  W1 ,34.55,08/09/88,200,452
CJ3421 ,10,  E4 ,34.50,03/05/88,120,213
FS6421 ,1,   A3 ,56.60,09/09/88,50,64
KL9008 ,4,   L9 ,124.90,07/02/88,40,46
KL9998 ,5,   G7 ,14.75,01/07/88,30,45
NU8099 ,5,   G3 ,24.50,03/05/88,35,66
```

dBASE allows fields within a record to be of differing types. They can be **NUMERIC**, **CHARACTER**, **DATE** or **LOGICAL**. There is a further type called a **MEMO** field, but its use falls outside the scope of this particular discussion. A numeric field contains numbers, a character field contains strings of characters, a date field contains a date in any one of a number of international formats and a logical field contains a symbol for a statement either being true or false. In the files shown in Figs 10.2 and 10.3 the fields are separated by commas.

Fig 10.3

```
AA1001 , Pins - 3/4 in
AA1002 , Pins - 1 inch
AA1003 , Pins - 2 inch
AA1005 , Pins - 3 inch
AB1002 , Nuts - small
AB1200 , Nuts - large
AC1002 , Reels - 1/4 inch
AC1003 , Reels - 1/2 inch
AF3005 , Spreaders - plastic
AG3006 , Spreaders - metal
AH5009 , Flatteners - plastic
BA1002 , Drawers - 2 inch
BA2005 , Drawers - 4 inch
BC3450 , Liners - plastic
BD4545 , Liners - wood
BE7878 , Liners - paper
```

```
BF2310 , String - long
BG1003 , String - very long
BH6754 , String - short
BJ1004 , Wire - short
CJ3421 , Wire - medium
FS6421 , Rods - metal
KL9008 , Rods - plastic
KL9998 , Rods - glass
NU8099 , Pails - metal
```

The program shown in Fig. 10.4 starts off with the **SET TALK OFF** and **SET ECHO OFF** commands that were in the first program. These can, in fact, be arranged to be defaults so that they do not need to be specified each time. **SET DATE BRITISH** is the instruction to display dates in the **DD/MM/YY** form rather than the American **MM/DD/YY** form. All text, by the way that starts with a * symbol or **&&** is treated as a comment. Normally only one database file can be worked on at a time, but in order to allow the use of two, or more, at once the memory can be divided up into separate "work areas". These are defined by the **SELECT** instruction. (This is similar to the file channels in BASIC.) In the first work area we are going to **USE** the file called **STOCK.DBF** and in the second we are going to *use* the other file, **CATALOG.DBF**. The word **USE** calls the named database file into the work area. The manipulation of data takes place in whichever work area is currently **SELECT**ed. Next we come to a **DO WHILE** loop which is terminated in this language with **ENDDO**. For ease of reading you will notice that we indent instructions so that it becomes clearer to follow. The loop is preceded by the instruction to set a memory variable called **Response** to contain the character "Y". This seeds the loop - notice that this fulfils the rule mentioned in Chapter 9, p. 119. The loop proceeds while this variable has this value. Its value can change at the end of the program if the user wishes to investigate another stock item. The **IF EOF()** (End-Of-File) test is like the one used in BASIC to test whether the last record in the file has been reached. Database files tend to be treated as serial files although

Fig. 10.4

```
*This program relates the contents of two database files.
SET DATE BRITISH
SET TALK OFF
SET STATUS OFF
SET ECHO OFF
SELECT 1
USE STOCK
SELECT 2
USE CATALOG
SELECT 1
RESPONSE = "Y"
DO WHILE RESPONSE = "Y"
        IF EOF()
                CLOSE ALL
                RETURN
        ENDIF
        @ 4,26 SAY "Useful Components Ltd"
        @ 2,0 TO 22,79 DOUBLE
        @ 7,1 TO 7,78
        @ 10,20 SAY "Part No :" + REF
        SELECT 2
        LOCATE FOR CATNO = A->REF
        @ 10,45 SAY DESCRIPT
        SELECT 1
        @ 12,20 SAY "Sold in packs of "+ STR(PACKSOF)
        @ 14,20 SAY "Stored in Bin " + BIN
        @ 16,20 SAY "Cost price per pack " + STR(COST,5,2)

        @ 18,20 SAY "Last delivery was on " + DTOC(DELDATE)
        @ 20,5 SAY "Reorder Level :" + STR(REORDER)
        @ 20,40 SAY "No. of packs in stock :" + STR(INSTOCK)

        ?
        ?
        ACCEPT "Next one ? (Y/N) " TO RESPONSE
        IF UPPER(RESPONSE) = "N"
                CLOSE ALL
                RETURN
        ELSE
                RESPONSE = "Y"
                SKIP
        ENDIF
ENDDO
CLOSE ALL
RETURN
```

records can be accessed directly. **CLOSE ALL** will close all open files and **RETURN** means a return to the program which called this one or to the main dBASE screen. The various @ **SAY** statements will define the position on the screen in terms of row and column where the text that follows will be displayed. The statement

> @ **10,20 SAY "Part No :" + Ref**

is the instruction to display the characters in quotes starting at row 10 column 20. The contents of the quotes are to be followed by the contents of the field called **REF** from the current record. The @ **2,0 TO 22,79 DOUBLE** is the instruction to draw a box, whose top left-hand corner and bottom right-hand corner references are quoted, in double thickness lines. The result is shown in Fig. 10.5.

Fig 10.5 *A typical screen produced by the program in Fig. 10.4*

```
┌──────────────────────────────────────────────────────┐
│                  Useful Components Ltd                 │
│                                                        │
│                                                        │
│        Part No:AA1001            Pins - 3/4 in         │
│                                                        │
│        Sold in packs of          10                    │
│                                                        │
│        Stored in Bin P1                                │
│                                                        │
│        Cost price per pack  2.35                       │
│                                                        │
│        Last delivery was on 14/07/88                   │
│  Reorder Level:  250      No of packs in stock : 344   │
└──────────────────────────────────────────────────────┘
Next One ? (Y/N)
```

The **LOCATE** instruction looks for a field called **CATNO** in the currently selected database that contains the same characters as the field called **REF** in the other database. Then the contents of the **DESCRIPT** field are displayed and the other database is used to display the contents of every field. Because the field called **PACKSOF** is numeric it must be converted into a string so that it can be displayed - using the **STR** function which is the same as that in BASIC. The **DTOC** function converts a date into characters again so that it might be displayed. **ACCEPT** operates in a similar manner to **INPUT** and asks for a character to be keyed in. The **UPPER** function automatically converts whatever is typed into upper case so that "n" becomes "N" and "y" becomes "Y". If the response is "Y" so that the next record in sequence is to be examined then the **SKIP** instruction takes you on to the next record. By this mechanism the file is examined record by record until the required one is found. When the response is "N" the files are closed and you are returned to the main screen or the program that called this one.

10.4 dBASE MENUS

One of the features of dBASE is that you can use it to create menus on the screen that give you the opportunity to select from a suite of programs by one single key depression. This makes the program particularly simple for non-computer people to use.

Fig. 10.6 shows a program that creates a menu and allows selection from it. Fig. 10.7 shows the menu screen seen by the operator.

Fig 10.6

```
* MENU Program - allows selection of programs
SET TALK OFF
SET STATUS OFF
SET ECHO OFF
SET DATE BRITISH
Screen = .T.
DO WHILE .T.
          IF Screen
          CLEAR
          ENDIF
          Choice = " "
          @ 2,30 say "Happy Valley Video Club"
          @ 3,30 say "-----------------------"
```

```
a 5,38 say "MENU"
a 7,6  say "A) Add a new member"
a 7,40 say "B) Add new films to the library"
a 9,6 say "C) Delete films from the library"
a 9,40 say "D) Search for a film"
a 11,6 say "E) List of all library films"
a 11,40 say "F) Loan film to member"
a 13,6 say "G) Return film to library"
a 13,40 say "H) List of current films on loan"
a 15,6 SAY "I) List of films in stock"
a 15,40 say "J) Exit from system"
a 20,25 say "Press the letter of your choice ";
GET Choice PICTURE "!"
READ
Screen = .T.
DO case
          CASE Choice = "A"
          DO PROGR6B
          Screen = .T.
          CASE Choice = "B"
          DO PROGR6A
          Screen = .T.
          CASE Choice = "C"
          DO PROGR9
          Screen = .T.
          CASE Choice = "D"
          DO PROGR5
          Screen = .T.
          CASE choice = "E"
          DO MENU2
          Screen = .T.
          CASE Choice = "F"
          DO PROGR11
          Screen = .T.
          CASE Choice = "G"
          DO PROGR13
          Screen = .T.
          CASE Choice ="H"
          DO PROGR12
          Screen = .T.
          CASE Choice = "I"
          DO PROGR7A
          Screen = .T.
          CASE Choice = "J"
          CLEAR
          a 12,36 say "THE END"
          CLEAR ALL
```

134

```
                  RETURN
                  OTHERWISE
                  @ 23,5 SAY "Invalid screen option - please re-enter
                  menu selection"
                  Screen = .F.
          ENDCASE
ENDDO
RETURN
```

Fig 10.7

```
                    Happy Valley Video club
                    -----------------------


                              MENU

A) Add a new member             B) Add new films to the library

C) Delete films from the library   D) Search for a film

E) List all library films       F) Loan film to member

G) Return film to library       H) List of current films on loan

I) List of films in stock       J) Exit from system



               Press the letter of your choice ▓
```

The program consists of a series of **DO CASE** instructions which are simply the instructions to be carried out for various values of the variable called **CHOICE**. If this is equal to the character "D" then the program called **PROGR5** is executed. The dBASE instruction **DO** followed by a program name (all programs have a **.PRG** extension) means "load and execute the program called . . . ". The statement that says

GET Choice PICTURE "!"
READ

is the instruction to read from the screen (that is, it is expecting you to key in a letter that appears on the screen) and the **PICTURE "!"** defines that whatever you enter it will be converted into an uppercase character. The **OTHERWISE** statement tells the program what to do if anything but the inputs expected are keyed in. The variable called **SCREEN** is set either to logical true (**.T.**) or false (**.F.**) so that the statement

IF Screen

means if the value held by the variable is true proceed with the statement that follows.

10.5 INDEXING FILES

Although this is not intended to be a rigorous description of the dBASE programming language there is one very useful and important feature that is worth mentioning. It is the technique of *indexing* files of data. We have seen in the sections that refer to BASIC programming, and the manipulation of files using that language, that this is not always a simple matter. Using dBASE you can create files of data of the sort you have already seen and although you can sort these into order according to any field in the records you can also save a lot of space simply by creating one or more *index* files relating to the database file. For example, the stock file you have already seen used in the program shown in Fig. 10.4 can be indexed on price, number of items per pack or by date of last delivery. All an index file does is to create a list of the record numbers relating to the main file allowing it to be listed in a *specified order*. For example if there was a file that contained names and initials:

1. Charles, P.L.
2. Harrison, K.J.
3. Adamson, B.
4. Fredericks, F.V.
5. Chamberlain, S.C.
6. Middleton, D.C.M.
7. Garside, D.

then if it was indexed on the surname to an index file, file extension **.NDX**, that file would simply contain seven records containing the record numbers

1. 3
2. 5
3. 1
4. 4
5. 7
6. 2
7. 6

so that when the main file was listed according to the index file we would get

1. Adamson, B.
2. Chamberlain, S.C.
3. Charles, P.L.
4. Fredericks, F.V.
5. Garside, D.
6. Harrison, K.J.
7. Middleton, D.C.M.

It is a simple matter to create index files since all we have to do is to is perform the following set of instructions, for example

USE STOCK
INDEX ON COST TO STOCKIND1

will create an index file called **STOCKIND1.NDX** and if
you were then to list the file it would not be in order of
reference numbers, as appears in Fig. 10.2, but in order of
the contents of the fourth field, the **COST** field. You can
index on any of the fields and in fact on a combination
of fields so that if you said

USE STOCK
INDEX ON BIN+STR(COST6,2) TO STOCKIND2

you would have another index file, quite independent of
the first one, called **STOCKIND2.NDX**, so that if you listed
the file now you would have it in the order of bin number
and within that the prices of its contents in order as well.

10.6 FINALLY

By using the dBASE programming language you have access
to a very large number of powerful operations so that
complicated operations are accessible by simple key words.
dBASE is particularly good at providing reports from the
database files that can be very easily constructed with the
help of comprehensive menus.
 If you want to find out more about this language then
there are two books in the *Macmillan Modern Office* series
- *Easily into dBASE III PLUS* and *Easily into dBASE III
PLUS programming,* both by Peter Gosling.

CHAPTER 11

COBOL

11.1 INTRODUCTION

COBOL (COmmon Business Orientated Language) has its origins in the early days of electronic computing when most of then work done was centred around the production of payrolls, stock lists and accounting systems. It stems from the days when all input to a computer system was via the medium of punched cards and still, even when used on microcomputer systems, retains this punched card-orientated feel. It also, when examined closely, appears to be a very verbose language using words such as **ADD**, **SUBTRACT**, **MULTIPLY** and **DIVIDE** instead of the more common mathematical symbols, although the latest versions of the language provide a way of getting around this.

All COBOL programs (which are compiled before execution) are divided into four separate *divisions*. These are:

(1)   *The Identification Division* which provides the facts about the program identifying who wrote it and when. Any comments about the program are included in this division.

(2)   *The Environment Division* providing information regarding the particular computer system on which it is being run. It will also provide information regarding the amount of memory required and any special peripheral equipment, such as tape drives, which may be required. This division would contain statements such as

SELECT INPUTA ASSIGN TO DISK

which informs the system that the file called **INPUTA** will be stored on a magnetic disk as opposed to magnetic tape. This information is stored in a *paragraph* within this division headed **FILE CONTROL**.

(3)   *The Data Division* contains two sections: the **FILE SECTION** and the **WORKING STORAGE** section. The first of these defines the structure of the files by specifying the names to be assigned to each field of each record and the number and type of characters in each field. (For more detailed information about this see G.G.L.Wright, *Mastering Computers*, Chapter 5 and Roger Hutty, *Mastering COBOL Programming*.) The descriptions of each field are achieved by using the **PIC** or **PICTURE** keyword. For example

PIC 9(5) means 5 decimal digits.
PIC 9(5) V99 means a number with five digits before the decimal point, V, and two digits after it.
PIC ZZZZ9.99 means a decimal number in the range 9.99 to 99999.99. The **Z**s imply that any zeros in these positions are suppressed (floating zeros).
PIC X(4) means four alphanumeric characters - that is, any of the set A - Z, 0 - 9.
PIC A(6) means six alphabetic characters (That is A - Z only.)
PIC S99 means a number in the range -99 to +99 - the **S** signifies the presence of a sign (+ or -).

Remember that a file consists of a series of *records* each of which is made up of a series of *fields*. The **WORKING STORAGE SECTION** defines the variables and constants used in the program; again they are defined by **PIC** statements.

(4)   *The Procedure Division* specifies the actual processing to be carried out and uses words to instruct the computer to perform its various tasks. Because words are used instead of symbols the program reads rather like a stilted piece of English prose. Separate parts of the program are

referenced by *labels* so that a COBOL *sentence* can look like this

IF STOCK-IN-HAND IS LESS THAN 200 GOTO REORDER-STOCK

where REORDER-STOCK is a label attached to a particular routine in the program. Labels are easy to spot in a COBOL program as the section they are attached to is always indented from the label.

All COBOL programs must have these four divisions even if they are *empty*.

11.2 COBOL PROGRAM LAYOUT

Because the COBOL language was born in the days of the 80-column punched card the layout of each line of a program has to follow a set pattern. One card was used for each program line and a COBOL card is shown in Fig. 11.1.

Fig 11.1 *The 80-column punched card*

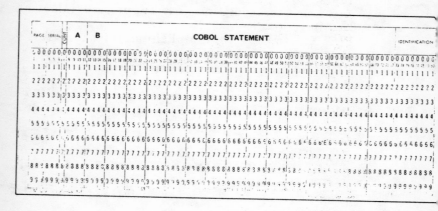

The first six characters of a program line are the *sequence number*. These can be numbered in any ascending order but increments of 10 are usually chosen. This allows for the insertion of new lines without the need to re-sequence the entire program. The seventh character is usually a blank, except when the line is a program comment. In this case a

* is placed in that position. Some versions of COBOL for PCs do not require sequence numbers (the compiler generates them), but they do require the first six characters to be blanks. The first example, shown in Fig. 11.2, is a simple COBOL program, the electricity bill again. You should notice that the *Identification Division* merely consists of the program name and that the *Environment Division* is empty. Note also that there are a lot of full stops in the program. They provide essential information to the compiler program and omission of any one of them would cause the compiler to generate program error messages. Notice also that labels are entered at column 8 and indented sections at column 12, refer to the printing on the card shown in Fig. 11.1.

Fig 11.2

```
0000010 IDENTIFICATION DIVISION.
0000020 PROGRAM ID. ELEC.
0000030 ENVIRONMENT DIVISION.
0000040 DATA DIVISION.
0000050 WORKING-STORAGE SECTION.
0000060 77 UNITS        PIC 9(5).
0000070 77 COST         PIC 9(5)V99.
0000080 77 EDITED-COST PIC ZZZZ9.99.
0000090 PROCEDURE DIVISION.
0000100 INPUT-UNITS
0000110     DISPLAY "TYPE IN UNITS OF ELECTRICITY USED".
0000120     ACCEPT UNITS.
0000130     IF UNITS <= 150
0000140         GO TO CALCULATE-COST
0000150     ELSE
0000160         GO TO AMEND-UNITS.
0000170 CALCULATE-COST.
0000180     MULTIPLY UNITS BY 0.07 GIVING COST.
0000190     IF COST IS LESS THAN 3.64
0000200         GO TO REVIEW-COST
0000210     ELSE
0000220         GO TO EXTEND-COST.
0000230 REVIEW-COST.
0000240     MOVE 3.64 TO COST.
0000250 EXTEND-COST.
0000260     ADD 3.25 TO COST.
0000270     MULTIPLY 1.15 BY COST.
0000280     MOVE COST TO EDITED-COST.
0000290     DISPLAY "£" EDITED-COST.
0000300     STOP RUN.
0000310 AMEND-UNITS.
0000320     SUBTRACT 150 FROM UNITS.
0000330     COMPUTE COST = (UNITS*0.05) + 10.5
0000340     GO TO EXTEND-COST.
```

Program outline: Line 130 uses the <= symbols for "less than or equal to" whereas line 190 uses words instead. Both are equally acceptable. Line 240 uses the word MOVE which is the equivalent of LET COST = 3.64 in BASIC. Line 270, which says MULTIPLY 1.15 BY COST, is the equivalent of the BASIC statement COST = COST * 1.15. If the word COMPUTE is used, as in line 330, then arithmetic symbols may be used. It saves using more complicated COBOL statements involving MOVE, MULTIPLY, ADD and GIVING: MULTIPLY UNITS BY .05 GIVING UNITS-COST and ADD UNITS-COST TO 10.5 GIVING COST. ACCEPT means that data is to be accepted from the keyboard and DISPLAY means that the named items are to be displayed on the screen.

11.3 A COBOL PROGRAM HANDLING FILES

COBOL is a language that is very heavily committed to handling large quantities of data which will be stored on tape or disk files. The amount of computation in most COBOL programs is relatively small, but the manipulation of that data is considerable. In particular it should be noted that the program shown in Fig. 11.3 is split up into clearly defined sections, called *paragraphs*, thus improving the clarity of the program for a reader. This program takes a series of fields in from a file and then sorts them in memory using the *shell sort* method described earlier and illustrated in BASIC in Fig. 4.7.

Fig. 11.3

```
000010 IDENTIFICATION DIVISION.
000020 PROGRAM I.D.SORTER.
000030 AUTHOR D.CHAPMAN.
000040 ENVIRONMENT DIVISION.
000050 INPUT-OUTPUT SECTION.
000060 FILE CONTROL.
000070    SELECT FILE1 ASSIGN TO DISK
000080 DATA DIVISION.
000090 FD FILE1.
000100 01 INREC.
000110    02 INKEY PIC X(4).
000120    02 FILLER PIC X(52).
000130 WORKING STORAGE SECTION.
000140 01 SORT-CONTROL.
000150    02 I PIC 9(5).
000160    02 J PIC 9(5).
000170    02 K PIC 9(5).
000180    02 L PIC 9(5).
000190    02 M PIC 9(5).
000200    02 N PIC 9(5).
000210 01 HOLD-TABLE.
000220    02 IN-FIELD OCCURS 250 TIMES.
000230       03 KEY1 PIC X(4).
000240       03 FILLER PIC X(52).
000250 01 ITEM-STORE PIC X(56).
```

```
000260 PROCEDURE DIVISION.
000270 BEGIN.
000280     OPEN INPUT FILE1.
000290     MOVE 1 TO N.
000300 READIT.
000310     READ FILE1 AT END GO TO SORTIT.
000320     MOVE INREC TO INFIELD(N).
000330     ADD 1 TO N.
000340     GO TO READIT.
000350 SORTIT.
000360     SUBTRACT 1 FROM N.
000370     CLOSE FILE1.
000380     MOVE N TO M.
000390 SORT1.
000400     DIVIDE 2 INTO M.
000410     IF M EQUALS 0
000420         GO TO SORT5.
000430     SUBTRACT M FROM N GIVING K.
000440     MOVE 1 TO J.
000450 SORT2.
000460     MOVE J TO I.
000470 SORT3.
000480     ADD I TO M GIVING L.
000490     IF KEY (I) IS SMALLER THAN KEY1(L)
000500         GO TO SORT4.
000510     IF KEY (I) EQUALS KEY1(L)
000520         GO TO SORT4.
000530     MOVE IN-FIELD (L) TO ITEM-STORE.
000540     MOVE IN-FIELD (I) TO INFIELD (L).
000550     MOVE ITEM-STORE TO INFIELD (I).
000560     SUBTRACT M FROM I.
000570     IF I IS GREATER THAN 0
000580         GO TO SORT3.
000590 SORT4.
000600     ADD 1 TO J.
000610     IF K IS SMALLER THAN J
000620         GO TO SORT2.
000630 SORT5.
000640     OPEN OUTPUT FILE1.
000650     MOVE 1 TO J.
000660 SORT6.
000670     MOVE IN-FIELD (J) TO INREC.
000680     WRITE INREC.
000690     ADD 1 TO,J.
000700     IF J IS GREATER THAN N
000710         GO TO FINISH.
000720     GO TO SORT6.
000730 FINISH.
000740     CLOSE FILE1.
000750     STOP RUN.
```

Program outline: The File Control section states that there is to be a file called FILE1 and it is to be a disk file. The FD section states that the records, each called INREC, are

divided into two fields - INKEY and FILLER. INKEY will contain four alphanumeric characters and FILLER, the name given to any elementary item which cannot be referred to explicitly, but which contains 52 alphanumeric characters. The variables in the program are called I, J, K, L, M and N and they are each numerics of up to nine digits. IN-FIELD is a subscripted variable, a list, which can contain up to 250 items. This is the COBOL equivalent of the DIM statement in BASIC. Each element of the list contains two fields called KEY1 and FILLER matching the fields of each record on the file. Finally there is a record called ITEM-STORE which can hold 56 alphanumeric characters. The Procedure Division starts with the instruction to open the file and assign the value 1 to the variable called N. The READIT set of instructions are to read the records one at a time and allocate them into successive records in the list IN-FIELD. When the last record has been read we go to the SORTIT paragraph, reduce the value of N by one, close the file and set the variable M to take the value of N. The rest of the program is the shell sort routine to sort the contents of the list IN-FIELD. When the list has been sorted on the key to the record called KEY1 then the sorted list is written back to the original file from IN-FIELD. Notice how it is possible with COBOL to read in large pieces of data, irrespective of what that data might be, and examine only part of it. Hence the use of FILLER which is really saying that we are interested only in the first four characters of the record as that is the part of the record we are going to use as our sort key. A point to note is in the instruction on line 000400 which says

DIVIDE 2 INTO M

and because in line 000190 we have defined M as being an integer (whole number) with up to five digits the result of the division will be a whole number, which is what we want.

PASCAL

12.1 INTRODUCTION

Here, for once, we have a computer language whose name
is not an acronym. It is a language designed in 1970 and
named after the seventeenth century French mathematician
Blaise Pascal, inventor of one of the earliest mechanical
calculating machines. It is a development of an earlier
language, ALGOL (**ALGO**rithmic Language) whose name
implies that it is based on a more organised and
mathematically orientated approach to programming than
other languages. In fact, the mathematical aspect refers to
the ideas relating to the proofs of theorems rather than the
mathematics of computation. The whole concept of the
language is the *structural* approach to the solution of a
problem. Such an approach not only makes it easier to
write the program but also improves the clarity for an
outsider who may have to take over the development of
them program from the original author.

Programs written in Pascal, or any other structured
language, are notable by their lack of **GOTO** statements
which tend to obscure the understanding of programs
written in more loosely organised languages. Writing a
computer program should always be approached in a *top-
down* manner. This means that the development of the
program should go from the general (top) to the particular
(down). This technique was shown in the development of a
program in Chapter 8. In that example the solution started
with a generalised flowchart which was then refined
further and further until a detailed flowchart and the
complete program emerged. Structured languages take away
the need for detailed flowcharts as is shown in an example
such as that in Chapter 1 on p. 5.

12.2 PASCAL INSTRUCTIONS

A structured language such as Pascal generally contains *six* types of instructions and these are

(1)   FOR loops as in BASIC
(2)   REPEAT/UNTIL loops
(3)   WHILE loops as in GWBASIC
(4)   decision instructions of the IF . . . THEN . . . ELSE . . . type
(5)   multiple decisions
(6)   PROCEDURES or subprograms

A set of instructions such as these should be quite adequate for a wide range of applications since they can be combined in three possible ways

(1)   *Sequential* instructions, as in a series of arithmetic operations.
(2)   *Subordinate* operations - selected loops of instructions embedded within other operations.
(3)   Procedures that are *freestanding* in the sense that they can be written separately. Hence this approach is ideal for creating programs in a modular manner. The concept of a procedure is found in both COBOL and the dBASE III PLUS programming language.

A very easy-to-follow example of how this works and how widely applicable the concept of structuring is to a non-computing activity is shown in Fig. 12.1. Just try to do the same thing in BASIC or COBOL and see how long it is before you get stuck! Notice that nowhere is there a **GOTO** instruction.

12.3 A BINARY SEARCH PROGRAM

The BASIC program listed in Fig. 12.2 uses a technique called a *binary search* to locate a particular element of a sorted list. Initially the list is divided into two equal parts, an upper part and a lower part. The number being located is tested against the number in the middle of the, list. The result of this test shows whether the number exists in the upper or the lower half of the list. Once this has been established the relevant half is again subdivided, tested and then halved again until the position of the number being searched for is finally located. The technique would be of

Fig 12.1 *A typical problem analysis in Pascal*

A football manager's approach to problem analysis and the stored program concept

A programmer's job is something like a football manager's. The manager must inculcate certain concepts into his players so that when a game starts they play good football without further interference from him.

His job is to analyse the problem (football) and formulate a set of rules for play, after which he must 'program' his players with these rules by training and coaching sessions.

The following 'program' is based on a somewhat simplified analysis of the game. It is in some ways more specific than a coach would be but its purpose is to illustrate good problem analysis using fundamental concepts.

```
REMARK Football manager's instructions to his players
FOR half = one TO two
  REPEAT
    WHILE the ball is in play
      IF opponents have ball THEN
        play in defensive positions
      ELSE
        REPEAT
          pass safely to team-mate
        UNTIL good attacking opportunity occurs
        EXECUTE attack
      ENDIF
    ENDWHILE
```

```
    UNTIL half time or final whistle
    leave the field and go to dressing room
  NEXT half
STOP
PROCEDURE attack
  REPEAT
    IF you have the ball THEN
      keep moving forward or pass
    ELSE
      run into space to receive a pass
    ENDIF
  UNTIL ball is in penalty area AND shot is possible
  shoot
ENDPROC
END
```

Note All structures must be opened and closed.

Opening keyword	Closing keyword
FOR	NEXT
REPEAT	UNTIL
WHILE	ENDWHILE
IF	ENDIF
PROCEDURE	ENDPROC

What happens between the opening and closing keywords is the content of that structure. Structures may be properly 'nested' or they may follow in sequence.

---

use, for example, if a telephone number was being searched for if the directory of numbers was in ascending order. A linear search from start to finish in a list of any size will always take an unreasonable time since each search starts at the beginning of the list and proceeds entry by entry until a match is found. If the number does not exist in the list then every number in the entire list has to be tested.

Fig 12.2

```
10 DIM A(100)
20 GOSUB 180
30 INPUT "Number to be searched for :";V
40 L=1
50 U=I-1
60 F=U
70 IF L<=U AND A(F)<>V THEN 90
80 GOTO 150
90 IF A(F)>V THEN 120
100 L=F+1
110 GOTO 130
120 U=F-1
130 F=INT((U+L)/2)
140 GOTO 70
150 IF A(F)<>V THEN PRINT "Not found":STOP
160 PRINT A(F);"Found"
170 STOP
180 FOR I=1 TO 100
190 READ A(I)
200 IF A(I)=999 THEN RETURN
210 NEXT I
```

```
220 DATA 3,6,7,8,9,12,21,22,34,44,55,56,
57,59,60,62,63,70,76,77
230 DATA 90,123,134,156,223,234,247,267,288,
299,300,321,322,500
240 DATA 999
```

Such a description is easy to follow in words and a language which allows us to put these words into its appropriate keywords has many obvious advantages. The example in Fig. 12.2 is difficult to follow as it tends to meander all over the place. The same program in Pascal shown in Fig. 12.3 is far easier to follow. No wonder Pascal programmers talk about "spaghetti" programming!

Fig 12.3

```
program BSEARCH;

var
LIST:array[1..100] of integer;
VAL:integer;
FOUND:integer;
LOW:integer;
HIGH:integer;
I: integer;
X: integer;
begin
        writeln ('Enter numbers one at a time - terminate
        with 999');
                begin
                I:=1;
                repeat
                write('Next number: ');
                readln (X);
                LIST[I]:=X;
                I:=I+1
                until X=999
                end;
        write ('Input number to be located: ');
        readln (VAL);
        LOW:=1;
        HIGH:=I-1;
        FOUND:=HIGH;
                while ((LOW <= HIGH) and (LIST[FOUND] <>
                VAL)) do
                begin
                if LIST[FOUND]>VAL then
                HIGH:=FOUND-1
                else LOW:=FOUND+1;
                FOUND:=(HIGH+LOW) div 2;
                end;
        begin
        if LIST[FOUND]<>VAL then
```

```
            writeln ('Not found')
            else writeln(LIST[FOUND],' Found!');
            write ('Press <Enter> to continue');
            readln;
            end;

    end.
```

Program outline: This program performs the binary search and uses an array called LIST to store the numbers, whose input is terminated by 999 just as in the BASIC program. Notice that it uses a REPEAT UNTIL statement as well as a DO . . . WHILE, or rather a WHILE . . . DO, construction to force the program into a loop. The "writeln" command will write the specified output to the screen and move the cursor to the start of the next line. The "write" command does the same except that it leaves the cursor after the last item displayed. The last two lines of the program cause the program to pause until the RETURN key is pressed. "div" is used in this program instead of the more usual "/" sign for division because "div" will only return the integer part of the quotient - which is what is required in this program. Other things to notice are the use of := instead of the more usual = symbol. This makes it easier to relate to the structured approach to programming where the symbol is used to stand for "takes the value of". You should notice that each line of program terminates in a ; character and the program end is denoted by a full stop . character. The program commences with a series of "declarations". These consist of the program name and the names of the constants and variables being used. The variables are "typed" - a real variable being a floating point variable, ones which have a fractional part and an exponent (12.456×10^3, for example). An integer variable will be stored as a whole number. The version of Pascal used for the production of this chapter is Turbo Pascal® 5 and this supports a number of different data types: byte, shortinteger, integer, word, longinteger, real, single precision, double precision, extended which take up from one to ten bytes of storage.

12.4 THE ELECTRICITY BILL PROGRAM

The next program is our electricity bill again but written in a far clearer manner as Fig. 12.4 shows.

Fig 12.4

```
program ELECTRICITYBILL;

const    BASERATE = 7;
         LOWRATE = 5;
         MINCHARGE = 325;
         STANDINGCHARGE = 325;
         VATRATE = 15;

var
          UNITS : integer;
          CHARGE : real;

begin
         write ('Enter number of units used:');
         readln (UNITS);
         if UNITS <= 150 then CHARGE := UNITS * BASERATE else

         CHARGE := 150 * BASERATE + (UNITS - 150) * LOWRATE;
         if CHARGE < MINCHARGE then CHARGE := MINCHARGE;
         CHARGE := ((CHARGE + STANDINGCHARGE) * (VATRATE/100
+ 1))/100;

         writeln ('Charges are : ',CHARGE);
         write ('Press <Enter> to continue.');
         readln;
end.
```

Program outline: The program is quite easy to follow as it matches the program shown on p. 5.

Fig. 12.5 shows the Turbo Pascal screen from which you can enter, edit, compile and run your Pascal program. The options run across the top of the screen in the manner of many other programs and it is easy and very fast to use. When you run a program you are returned to the DOS screen. Compilation is either to memory ready to run or to disk where the compiled program is stored with a .EXE extension ready to run completely outside the Turbo Pascal environment.

For further detailed reading regarding the writing of Pascal programs you are referred to *Mastering Pascal Programming* by Eric Huggins.

12.5 A TURBO PASCAL PROGRAM USING FILES

The last program in this chapter shows how Pascal uses files and in addition it shows how the language is used to operate at bit level on a file. What it does is to strip out all spurious characters from a file by looking at the file and replacing any character that has an ASCII value of less than 32 or greater than 126; these are stripped out and replaced by a space which has an ASCII value of 32 (see Fig. 12.6).

Fig 12.5 *The Turbo Pascal Main Screen*

```
   File    Edit    Run    Compile   Options   Debug   Break/watch
                                    Edit
       Line 1      Col 1   Insert Indent        Unindent   B:ELEC.PAS
program ELECTRICITYBILL;

const BASERATE = 7;
      LOWRATE = 5;
      MINCHARGE = 325;
      STANDINGCHARGE = 325;
      VATRATE = 15;
var
      UNITS : integer;
      CHARGE : real;

begin
write ('Enter number of units used:');
readln (UNITS);
if UNITS <= 150 then CHARGE := UNITS * BASERATE else
CHARGE := 150 * BASERATE + (UNITS - 150) * LOWRATE;
if CHARGE < MINCHARGE then CHARGE := MINCHARGE;
CHARGE := (CHARGE + STANDINGCHARGE) * (VATRATE/100 + 1)/100;
                              Watch
```

F1-Help F5-Zoom F6-Switch F7-Trace F8-Step F9-Make F10-Menu

Fig 12.6

```
program Hex2Txt;
{Program by Frank Hatfull - strips all unwanted characters
from a text file}


Const
        PathLength = 65;

Type
        FileName   = String[PathLength];

Var
        MainFileName      : FileName;
        Outfilename       : FileName;
        MainFile          : text;
        OutFile           : text;

Function Open(var fp:text; name: Filename): boolean;
begin
        Assign(fp,Name);
        Assign(OutFile,Outfilename);
        reset(fp);
        rewrite(Outfile);
        {SI-}
```

```
            If IOresult <> 0 then
          begin
                  Open := False;
                  close(fp);
          end
          else
                  Open := True;
          {SI+}
          end { Open };

Procedure OpenMain;
begin
          If ParamCount  < 2 then
          begin
                  Write('Enter  INPUT  filename      --->
                  ');
                  readln(MainFileName);
                  Writeln;
                  Write('Enter  OUTPUT filename      --->
                  ');
                  readln(OUTFileName);
                  Writeln;
          end
          else
          begin
                  MainFileName := ParamStr(1);
                  OutFileName  := ParamStr(2);
          end;

          If Not Open(MainFile,MainFileName) Then
          begin
                  Writeln('ERROR -- File not found:  ');
                  Halt;
                  end;

          end {Open Main};


          Procedure ProcessFile;
          var
                  InChar : char;

                  begin  {Process File}

                  Write('Converting . . . ');
                  read(MainFile,InChar);

                  while not eof(mainfile)  do
                  begin

                          If ( ORD(InChar) < 32  ) OR (
                          ORD(InChar) > 126) then
                          InChar := CHR(32);

                          Write(OutFile,InChar);
```

```
                    Read(Mainfile,InChar);

            end;

            WriteLn;
            WriteLn('******    Conversion    Completed
            ******');

            close(MainFile);
            end {Process File};


     BEGIN
     Writeln ;
     Writeln ('                    Cherry Pie Computing - File
     Conversion ') ;
     Writeln ;
     OpenMain;

     ProcessFile;

     END.
```

Program outline: This program strips any non-printing characters from a text file. It uses a number of Pascal features: functions and procedures (which are similar to subroutines in BASIC) and a number of Pascal standard functions. The declaration of "type" allows you to define your own data types, in this case FILENAME is defined as containing a string of up to 65 characters. The program examines every character in the input string from the named file to see if its ASCII value lies in the range from 0 to 126. If it does then that character is replaced with a blank (ASCII 32). A number of Pascal functions are used in this program.
They are:

Ord,	Returns the ordinal number of an ordinal type value
Paramstr,	Returns a specified command line parameter
Paramcount,	Returns the number of parameters passed to the program from the command line
Assign,	Assigns the name of a file to a file variable
Reset,	Opens an existing file

Rewrite,	Creates and opens a new file
IOResult,	Returns an integer that is the status of the last I/O operation performed
{SI-},	Switches I/O checking off in order to trap errors with IOResult
{SI+},	Switches I/O checking on

C

13.1 INTRODUCTION

The great advantage of using C as a programming language is that it is a *portable* language. This means that a program written in C can be run on a variety of computers, not just PCs, and will run without any modification. This is not the case with the other languages described in this book. It is a structured language capable of being written in modules and it is, as with COBOL, Pascal and PROLOG, a language which can produce a compiled file, with a .EXE extension, so that it can be run directly from the operating system. C is used often used for what is called *systems programming* and such things as compilers for other languages and software packages are written in the language. The particular version of C used to produce the examples in this chapter is Turbo C®. The screen presented to you when using this version of the C language is the same as that displayed when you are using Turbo Pascal.

C is not a language that lends itself very well to writing applications programs such as accounting systems, structural analysis or complex mathematical operations. Not only that but C itself has no specific input and output routines. It has to make calls on libraries of routines to perform these. Such a library is the one at the head of the programs that follow; the library called **stdio.h**. Other libraries are called in for specific purposes such as **math.h** that contains all the mathematical functions, **float.h** that contains the parameters for floating point routines and **graphics.h** that contains the graphics routines. The standard reference on the C language is *The C Programming Language* by Kernighan and Richie.

13.2 A PROGRAM IN C

A program in C will in general start with an instruction that reads

#include <stdio.h>

which is a directive to the translation program that it needs to use information stored in a file called **stdio.h**. Following this the program proper commences with

main()

and the program instructions are written between a pair of curly brackets { and }. A simple C program would therefore be

```
#include<stdio.h>

main()
   {
   printf("This is a C program\n");
   }
```

The \n in the **printf** statement is called an *escape sequence* and is the instruction to move the cursor to a new line. In addition the characters that are printed appear on the screen. If **fprintf** is used instead of **printf** then the characters are printed out to a file, called **stdprn** in this case. As with Pascal programs, declarations are made declaring the type of any variables used within the program. A range of data types are available ranging from **unsigned char** that takes up one byte to **long double** that requires ten bytes of storage.

C uses several special characters such as the *decrement operator* -- and the *increment operator* ++. These subtract 1 and add 1 respectively to a variable so that a statement such as

count--;

means "reduce the value held in **count** by one and store the new value in **count**".

You can also say

--count;

and the two versions are *not the same.*

A program showing the effect of these operators is shown in Fig. 13.1 where you should notice the declaration of the variables as integers, the use of **fprintf** with the printer definition, **stdprn**, in the brackets. The **%d** is a format string, in this case defining *integer* format. Examples of other formats are %f for floating point format, %s for a string of characters and %c for a single character.

Fig 13.1

```
#include <stdio.h>

main()
{
        int a,b,c,d;
        a=6;
        b=a--;
        d=6;
        c=--d;
        fprintf(stdprn,"%d \n",b);
        fprintf(stdprn,"%d \n",c);
        a=6;
        d=6;
        b=a++;
        c=++d;
        fprintf(stdprn,"%d \n",b);
        fprintf(stdprn,"%d \n",c);
}
```

Program outline: When this program is run the output is

6
5
6
7

indicating that only --d has the effect of showing the decrement and ++d has the effect of showing the increment. It means that the "prefix" sign performs the decrementing or incrementing after the assignment is made and the "postfix" sign performs it before the assignment is made. You can write instruction lines such as

a = b + b++

and

a = a + ++b

both of which have different outcomes.

13.3 THE ELECTRICITY BILL AGAIN

The electricity bill program is very simple to transcribe into the C language from the structured flowchart on p. 5 and the appropriate program is shown in Fig. 13.2.

Fig. 13.2

```
#include <stdio.h>

main()
{
        int units;
        float cost;

        printf("Enter number of units used :");
        scanf("%d",&units);
        if(units<=150)
                cost=units*.07;
        else
                cost=10.5+(units-150)*.05;
        if (cost < 3.64)
                cost=3.64;
                cost=(cost+3.25)*1.15;
        fprintf(stdprn,"\n %f",cost);
}
```

Program notes: The scanf command is the instruction to receive data from the keyboard. Notice that the name of the numeric variable read in is prefixed by a & symbol. Character variables do not need prefixing by this symbol. The very last instruction directs that the following data be written on a new line in floating point format. The if . . . else . . . test and instructions are very similar to those in other languages. C does, however, have a "goto" instruction. You should note the positions of the ; characters that terminate an instruction. In the "if" test all the usual arithmetic tests are available except that = = replaces = when you write

if (cost = = 3.45)

for example. The symbols != stand for "not equal".

13.4 LOOPS IN C

There are two loops forms that are used in the C programming language. The first of these is similar to the BASIC FOR . . . NEXT . . . command and a program that uses this is shown in Fig. 13.3.

Fig. 13.3

```
#include <stdio.h>;

main()
{
        int index;
        for (index = 1; index <=15; index++)
        fprintf(stdprn,"%2d \n",index);
}
```

Program notes: Notice here how the increment characters, ++, are used to increment the counter. All the program does is to print the numbers 1 to 15, but it does it with the minimum of commands.

Fig. 13.4 provides a program that performs in the same way as the one in Fig. 13.3 except that it uses a **do . . . while** loop.

Fig 13.4

```
#include <stdio.h>;

main()
{
        int index;
        index=1;
        do{
        fprintf(stdprn,"%2d \n",index);
        index++;
        }while (index<16);
}
```

Program outline: Notice in this that the instructions to be performed within the loop are enclosed in a further pair of {} brackets with the on-going test of the variable called index appearing outside the loop.

The program in Fig. 13.5 puts a series of random numbers into an array called **NUMS** and then proceeds to select the smallest and the largest from the list and calculate and print the average size of the numbers in the list.

Fig 13.5

```
#include <stdio.h>;
#include <stdlib.h>;
#include <time.h>;

main()
{
        float nums[50];
```

```
int i;
float small;
float large;
float av;
float total;
randomize();
for (i=1;i<50;i++)
nums[i]=random(1000)+1;
for (i=1;i<50;i++)
fprintf(stdprn,"Random Number : %f\n",nums[i]);
large=nums[1];
small=nums[1];
total = nums[1];
for (i=2;i<50;i++)
{ if(nums[i]>large)
  large=nums[i];
  if (nums[i]<small)
  small=nums[i];
  total = total +nums[i];
}
av=total/50.;
fprintf(stdprn,"Total is %f\n",total);
fprintf(stdprn,"smallest is %f\n",small);
fprintf(stdprn,"largest is %f\n",large);
fprintf(stdprn,"average is %f\n",av);
}
```

Program outline: You will notice that the random number generator is used in much the same way as in BASIC to generate a number in the range 1 to 1000. The "for" loop has to have a pair of {} brackets around the lines that follow it as you are only allowed one line after such a statement (there is no "next" to tell you where the loop ends as in BASIC).

PROLOG

14.1 INTRODUCTION

It was only quite recently that the author suddenly came to recognise one of the reasons why it was often difficult for people to come to terms with the computer. It was that in order to use a piece of software one needed to have some sort of expertise in a field related to that software before the computer and its software could be of any value at all. Even to use a word processor one needs to be able to type, or at least know one's way around a keyboard, and have a *real need* for the features offered by the program. Software in general could be described as solutions looking for problems to solve. If you have no problems, then you have no need for a computer.

Even ten or twelve years ago the computer was often the "showpiece" of an organisation and one was often faced with the task of "showing the Mayor the computer"! A very daunting task, since to show it was a ten-second job, but to demonstrate its power required some appreciation by the audience of the tasks it was performing. Because these were mainly sophisticated accounting or scientific operations simple games and examples had to be invented in order to trivialise the machine's functions so that the layman could understand something of what was going on.

Now, with the availability of knowledged-based systems a new kind of computing has appeared on the scene. Whereas previously computers had been used mainly for arithmetic calculations, "number crunching", or the manipulation of symbols as in a word processor, we can now use them to act as a source of "know-how". Not only that, but we can now do something which we were never able to do before. We can now ask the computer just *why it has produced its answer.*

In the United Kingdom the Alvey Committee (see Further Reading section) has been looking at expert systems - a slightly more evocative name for knowledge-based systems - since the late 1970s as has the British Computer Society. This latter organisation has come up with a definition that puts the concept of these programs into a nutshell:

"An expert system is regarded as the embodiment within a computer of a knowledge-based component from an expert skill in such a form that the system can offer intelligent advice or take an intelligent decision about a processing function. A desirable characteristic, which many would consider fundamental, is the capability of the system, on demand, to justify its own line of reasoning in a manner directly intelligible to the enquirer. The style adopted to attain these characteristics is rule-based programming."

Having spent many years as a teacher the author watched with interest while many so-called "teaching aids" came and went. In the 1960s there were teaching machines which, although based on sound theory, were never successful. One of the reasons why this was so was that the technology was not available at the time in order to make them work effectively. When the computer, and then the desktop micro-computer, appeared on the educational scene in the late 1970s all the previous work done on teaching machines was dusted off and the new technology was brought into action in order to implement the earlier teaching machine theories. But even with this new approach, the technique still did not catch on.

Despite the fact that these machines could now display graphs, draw pictures, play tunes and ask questions the programming involved in driving the system was based on a purely *algorithmic* approach to learning. This meant that if a question and answer session took place with the computer it was very rare that any deviation from a fixed set of answers was allowed. The STAF (Science Teacher's Authoring Facility) and the National Physical Laboratory's MICROTEXT systems were very flexible but, despite assertions to the contrary, required a certain amount of programming ability in order for the teacher to generate effective teaching programs. It is not surprising, therefore, that only those teachers who had been prepared to spend time getting to grips with the new technology made use of the systems. Not only that, but in order to allow for all the possible mistakes each student might make, the amount of programming needed to produce even a simple teaching program was out of all proportion to the quality of the end result. With the very sophisticated features offered by STAF and MICROTEXT it was possible to take some account of the possibility of a student having some wrong concept from the start and even allowed for mis-spellings in responses. But the systems still could easily be fooled.

What was really required was some system by which a human teacher could transfer his or her accumulated knowledge and experience to a computer in a form that required no computing experience at all so that in some way the computer would be able to make the same kind of assessments as the human teacher and be able to sense when a student had a real problem. Machines that operate algorithmically are very insensitive. However, if you can give a machine all the rules of thumb by which the teacher works then it can appear to have some sort of sensitivity.

The important phrase at the end of the last paragraph is "appear to have". No machine is ever likely to become inherently "clever" - the concept of Artificial Intelligence has been a sort of Holy Grail of computing for many years but despite all the hard work put into its development there seems little chance of achieving the purely "intelligent machine" for many years. No machine can ever be cleverer than whoever gave it the knowledge in the first place. If we can find some way of storing a collection of rules of thumb, known as "heuristics", and then testing these rules against known facts then we are on the way to achieving our expert system.

Before we go any further there is a point that must be made clear. There is a difference between the terms "knowledge-based system" and "expert system". A knowledge-based system is one which uses a body of knowledge - usually in the form of a set of rules - to make *inferences* about a given situation. For example, a set of rules, the knowledge base, can be kept concerning the possible things that can go wrong with a micro-computer. A user can explain the symptoms of a malfunctioning machine to the knowledge-based system which will then respond with a series of suggestions of what is wrong. Similarly, a knowledge base of medical facts can be used to diagnose an illness from a described set of symptoms.

The primary requirement of a knowledge-based system is *knowledge*. It is in the means of acquiring this knowledge that the definition of an expert system is derived. Knowledge can be obtained from a variety of sources. It can be found in reference books, in manuals, from personal experience or from asking someone else. If the someone else whom you choose to ask is an expert on a particular subject then your knowledge-based system is an expert system. But if your particular subject requires little knowledge but lots of skill, such as paper-hanging or making love, it is unlikely that your system would be much good and we are not talking about an expert system.

Knowledge-based systems can offer help in two ways. The first of these is in advisory capacity so that a system can be consulted about the building regulations or the rules governing Statutory Sick Pay. The other is where the accumulated "know-how" of a specialist in, say, company law or bridge design is conveyed to other people.

There must be very few fields of human activity that are governed solely by book-learning. A set of known and accepted facts obviously form the basis of the work of accountants, doctors, scientists and computer maintenance engineers and they are obviously very important. But in addition to this base of knowledge each profession has its set of heuristics. Medical diagnosis has been using these "head rules" for centuries. An accountant or an engineer with twenty years of experience is probably a better accountant or engineer than one straight out of university, despite the fact that they probably both possess the same amount of factual knowledge. It is *experience* in the form of these head rules, or rules of thumb, built up over the years which gives the edge to the older person.

So what does a heuristic look like? The answer is very simple, since they all begin with the keyword IF and use the keyword THEN. For example

   IF it is likely to rain
   THEN I will take a raincoat

or

   IF it is sunny
     and today is Saturday
   THEN we will go for a picnic

or even

IF a disk is loaded onto my computer
    and the computer is switched on
    and the disk contains a word processing program
    and the printer is connected
    and the printer is switched on
    and the printer is loaded with paper
THEN I can write a letter
    and print it out

The knowledge base contained within such a system will contain a series of rules of the type shown above and possibly a series of facts. These rules are tested against the answers to a series of questions which are generated by the system and a conclusion can be reached. When this conclusion is reached the system can be asked why it reached that particular conclusion and the rules used will be displayed. Existing rules contained in the knowledge base can be amended and new rules inserted in order to take account of changes of circumstance.

All this produces a crop of new jargon. Apart from "heuristics" we now have "knowledge engineers" who are the people who design knowledge-based systems. The rules and facts are stored in a "knowledge base" in the same way as data is stored in a database. An "Inference Engine" is used to drive the system. An Inference Engine is program written in a language such as PROLOG (PROgramming in LOGic) or LISP (LISt Processing). It is the PROLOG language, which can exist in a number of different versions, that will be described in this chapter. The version used here is TURBO PROLOG®.

When you combine an Inference Engine with suitable software interfaces in order to make a system simple to use and understand then you have a system "shell".

Before going any further it would be suitable to look in general terms at the way a knowledge-based system works. A more detailed examination is given later on in the book.

Suppose we have a series of rules that are related in the following way:

Rule 1 : IF A is true
     and B is true
    THEN C is true

Rule 2 : IF C is true
    THEN D is true

Rule 3 : IF D is true
    THEN E is true

Rule 4 : IF E is true
     and B is true
    THEN F is true

Rule 5 : IF F is true
    THEN G is true

Next, if we know that A and B are both true how do we show that G is true? There are two ways of doing this. The first is to proceed from the base of facts through the rules until we can show that what we want to prove true is, in fact, true. This is known as "forward chaining" and we use the knowledge we already possess to generate new knowledge. Thus we can add to our knowledge base. In this simple example we know from Rule 1 that if A and B are true then C must be true. Our knowledge base has now been extended. We can show the process by means of a series of statements as follows:

	Knowledge Base
Initially	{A,B}
Rule 1: A AND B --> C	{A,B,C}
Rule 2: C --> D	{A,B,C,D}
Rule 3: D --> E	{A,B,C,D,E}
Rule 4: B AND D --> F	{A,B,C,D,E,F}
Rule 5: F --> G	{A,B,C,D,E,F,G}

So we finally are able to deduce that G is in fact true. With forward chaining the ultimate goal of the reasoning may not be known. It is only by the continued application of the deductions made from the knowledge base that a final outcome may be arrived at.

The other way in which the truth of G can be established is by using "backward chaining" or "goal-directed" reasoning. In this method we know that our goal is G, knowing at the start that A and B are true. We then look back rule by rule to see what fact, or facts, have to be true in order for G to be true. The sequence of events is therefore

Goal	Rule examined next	Knowledge base
G true	Rule 5	{A,B}
F true	Rule 4	{A,B}
E AND B true	Rule 3	{A,B}
D true	Rule 2	{A,B}
C true	Rule 1	{A,B,C,D,E,F,G}

In each case we are saying, "what do we need to know in order to show that a statement is true?". So we see that if G is to be true, then F has to be true. If F is to be true then E and B are to be true. But B is known to be true. Then if F is to be true then D must be true. If D is to be true then C must be true. Finally - if B and C are true A must be true, which it is. Hence G must be true.

These rules can be stated in a different form if required in order to produce an "inference net". They can be stated as

G DEPENDS ON F AND E

F DEPENDS ON E AND B

E DEPENDS ON D

D DEPENDS ON C

C DEPENDS ON A AND B

which can be illustrated graphically as

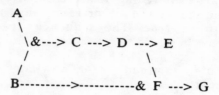

When knowledge-based systems are used all except the very simple ones use a mixture of both forward and backward chaining and rules can be used more than once during any examination of a knowledge base.

Constructing a knowledge-based system forces us to think in a totally new way. All of us who have been brought up to think algorithmically have to drop any attempt at that sort of approach to a problem. Not only that, but knowledge-based systems can depend on a different type of logic from that which says "the outcome of knowing this fact and that fact is . . . ". We can examine systems which say "if the chance of this fact being true is 0.5 and the chance of that fact being true is 0.3 then the probability of a particular outcome is . . . ". Various types of logic are used in knowledge-based systems from the simple classical logic which says that a statement is either true of false to those using "fuzzy" logic that relates the probability of certain truths with the probability of a particular outcome.

A knowledge-based system must first of all have some means by which knowledge can be represented. Secondly, there must be the "Inference Engine" which handles the logic and applies it to the knowledge base. In other words, there has to be a suitable way of representing the knowledge *symbolically* and a method of *manipulating* these symbols. The logic system that is applied to these symbols is known as the "inferencing logic".

14.2 LOGIC SYSTEMS

In general, there are three basic types of logic systems. The first of these is the classical "propositional" logic. This is the standard logic of mathematics using AND, OR, NOT, IMPLIES and IS EQUIVALENT TO. This logic system is probably the simplest to understand and was that used in the examples earlier in this chapter. The truth of a statement is affirmed by the truth of those statements related to it; so that a statement such as

If A AND B Then C

could represent

If water is in the kettle and it is switched on then the water will be heated

Where

A = [Water in the kettle]

B = [Kettle switched on]

C = [Water will be heated]

Classical logic allows us to manipulate logical statements so that we know that if A is true and B is false then the statement [A AND B] is false but the statement [A OR B] is true. *Truth tables* can therefore be established and made use of in this type of logic:

A	B	A AND B
True	False	False
False	True	False
True	True	True
False	False	False

Similarly

[A OR NOT B] is the same as NOT[NOT A AND B]

It is this type of logic that is used in conventional algorithmic programming of the type associated with all the programming languages discussed so far. And by using this logic simple heuristic rules can be developed and tested.

If predicate logic is used rather than propositional logic then

A = [Water in the kettle]

becomes

A = [Water]

B = [Kettle]

These units are called "objects" and a statement about an object is called a "predicate", so that the statement about water in the kettle can be written as

in_the kettle(water)

which is an assertion that water is in the kettle and can be either true or false. This could perhaps be better written as

in__the(water,kettle)

which is a two-part predicate which can also be either true or false. Predicate logic statements can be connected by the same AND, OR, NOT, IMPLIES and IS EQUIVALENT TO connectives used in propositional logic so that we can write

in__the(water,kettle) AND on(switch)

which can be either true or false. It could therefore be written as

in__the(A,B) AND on(C)

Knowledge stored in this way can be expressed in a *network*. As an example, the simple knowledge base

is__head__of(Jane,School)
part__of(Class,School)
part__of(Pupil,Class)
is__a(Roger,Pupil)
is__a(John,Teacher)
teaches(Teacher,Class)

can be illustrated by the network

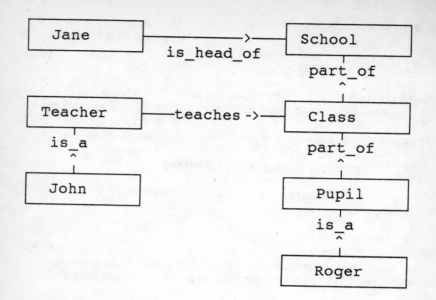

We can then proceed to make deductions about the system so that we can, for example, deduce that John is Roger's teacher, that Roger is taught by John and that Roger is one of the pupils in Jane's school.

It is this predicate logic that is used by PROLOG.

14.3 WHY USE PROLOG?

If we write down the decisions we have to make when buying a car we can produce a series of steps and decisions that seem to make a perfectly logical and satisfactory program in, say, BASIC. Such a program could look as shown in Fig. 14.1.

In that program the only piece of logic is in line 80 where it evaluates the truth of the three statements **M$="No"**, **O$="No"** and **C$="No"** and defines the outcome if any one of the first OR the second OR the third statements are true. This is not a very satisfactory way of going about this problem since the responses depend entirely on what is keyed in and not the *meaning* of what is keyed in. In other

words, if you keyed in **yes** as the answer to the first
question you would be told not to buy because the expected
answer was **Yes**. There clearly must be a better way of
doing it than this for this kind of problem and one of the
better ways is to write it in terms of knowledge rather
than data. PROLOG creates a knowledge base rather than
a data base as you will see.

Fig. 14.1

```
10 INPUT "Have you seen a car you like ";LIKE$
20 IF LIKE$="Yes" THEN 30 ELSE GOTO 170
30 INPUT "Is the car new or second-hand ";N$
40 IF N$="New" THEN 90
50 INPUT "Is it a low mileage car "; M$
60 INPUT "Is it a one-owner car ";O$
70 INPUT "Is it in good condition ";C$
80 IF (M$="No") OR (O$="No") OR (C$="No") THEN 170
90 INPUT "Is a good trade-in price offered ";T$
100 IF T$="Yes" THEN 110 ELSE 170
110 INPUT "Is the cash available ";CASH$
120 IF CASH$="Yes" THEN 190 ELSE 130
130 INPUT "Is HP available ";AVAIL$
140 IF AVAIL$= "Yes" THEN 150 ELSE 170
150 INPUT "Can you afford the HP charges ";AFFORD$
160 IF AFFORD$="Yes" THEN 190
170 PRINT "DON'T BUY IT!"
180 STOP
190 PRINT "Go ahead - buy it - Happy motoring!"
200 STOP
```

14.4 THE PROLOG APPROACH

A program written in Turbo Prolog to make deductions
from the facts mentioned on p. 171 looks like this

```
predicates

is_head_of(symbol,symbol)
part_of(symbol,symbol)
is_a(symbol,symbol)
teaches(symbol,symbol)
is_a_teacher_of(symbol,symbol)
```

```
clauses

is_a_teacher_of(Teachername,Pupilname) if
teaches(Teacher,Class) and
is_a(Pupilname,Pupil)and
is_a(Teachername,Teacher) and
part_of(Pupil,Class).

is_head_of(jane,school).

part_of(class,school).
part_of(pupil,class).

is_a(roger,pupil).
is_a(john,teacher).

teaches(teacher,class).
```

The first few lines of the program declare the general facts, called *predicates*; because PROLOG can handle symbols, lists, integers and other types of variable, we have to state what kind of variables we are using in the various predicates. This is similar to what we have to do in languages such as Pascal and C. In the predicate list are all the general relationships we intend to use. Following the predicates are the *clauses* that state the facts or rules. A fact is a property of an object or a relation between objects. *Objects* are enclosed within the brackets and *relations* are whatever precedes the brackets so that if we write

teaches(Teacher,Class)

the relation is **teaches** and the objects are **Teacher** and **Class**. Any object that commences with a capital letter is deemed to be a variable and any object starting with a lower case letter is a constant. Thus **roger** is a constant and **Pupilname** is a variable that can take one of a range of values. The first part of the clauses section states the facts that have to be true if the facts at the head of the clauses is to be true also, using **if** and **and**. In the above example the intention of the program is to find out who teaches who and this is done by declaring a *goal* in the form of a *query*. The query will be entered as

is__a__teacher__of(Who,What)

and PROLOG will respond by giving the solutions which are values for the variables **Who** and **What**. The solutions in this will be **john** and **roger**. The way that this works in Turbo PROLOG is shown next.

14.5 USING TURBO PROLOG

When you start the program you will be presented with a screen that contains four boxes as shown in Fig. 14.2. The PROLOG program is entered into the **Edit** box which acts as a simple word processor. You could, if you wished, enter the program via an external word processor save it with a **.PRO** extension as an ASCII file and then read it in to PROLOG. Having created the raw program you press the **Alt** and **R** keys and if there are no errors the prompt **Goal:** appears in the **Dialog** box. You key in your goal and PROLOG responds, hopefully, with the answer.

Fig 14.2 *The blank PROLOG screen*

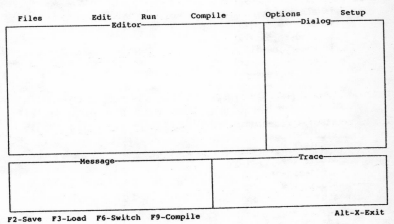

The next example is rather more adventurous and looks like this

```
predicates

is_head_of(symbol,symbol)
part_of(symbol,symbol)
is_a(symbol,symbol)
teaches(symbol,symbol)
teaches_maths_to(symbol,symbol)
studies(symbol,symbol)
specialises_in(symbol,symbol)

clauses

teaches_maths_to(Teachername,Pupilname) if
teaches(Teacher,Class) and
is_a(Pupilname,Pupil)and
is_a(Teachername,Teacher) and
specialises_in(Teachername,maths) and
studies(Pupilname,maths) and
part_of(Pupil,Class).

is_head_of(jane,school).

part_of(class,school).
part_of(pupil,class).

is_a(roger,pupil).
is_a(henry,pupil).
is_a(susan,pupil).
is_a(mary,pupil).
is_a(john,teacher).
is_a(joan,teacher).
is_a(brenda,teacher).
teaches(teacher,class).

studies(roger,maths).
studies(roger,french).
studies(roger,english).
studies(henry,maths).
studies(henry,english).
studies(susan,french).
studies(susan,english).

specialises_in(john,maths).
```

We can use this program to discover who teaches maths to whom. This is done by supplying the query

    teaches__maths__to(john,What)

in order to find the names of the pupils who are taught maths by John and by

    teaches__maths__to(Who,What)

to find a list of the maths teachers, if there was more than one, and the maths students. Both these goals and the final screen display are shown in Fig. 14.3.

Fig 14.3 *Screen after running a PROLOG program twice*

```
 Files        Edit         Run         Compile         Options    Setup
─────────────────Editor─────────────────              ───────────Dialog───────
  Line 3    Col 1   B:SCHOOL3.PRO    Indent Insert   Goal: teaches_maths_
predicates                                           to(john,What)
                                                     What=roger
is_head_of_(symbol,symbol)                           What=henry
part_of(symbol,symbol)                               2 Solutions
is_a(symbol,symbol)                                  Goal: teaches_maths_
teaches_maths_to(symbol,symbol)                      to(Who,What)
studies(symbol,symbol)                               Who=john, What=roger
specialises_in(symbol,symbol)                        Who=john, What=henry
                                                     2 Solutions
clauses

teaches_maths_to(Teachername,Pupilname) if
teaches(Teacher,Class)and
─────────────────Message─────────────────            ──────────Trace──────────
specialises_in
is_a
teaches_maths_to
is_a

F2-Save F3-Load F5-Zoom F6-Next F8-Previous goal Shift-F10-Resize F10-Goal
```

The third program relating to this base of information is shown next

```
predicates

is_head_of(symbol,symbol)
part_of(symbol,symbol)
is_a(symbol,symbol)
teaches(symbol,symbol)
is_a_pupil_of(symbol,symbol)

clauses

is_a_pupil_of(Teachername,Pupilname) if
is_head_of(Teachername,School) and
part_of(Class,School)and
part_of(Pupil,Class)and
is_a(Pupilname,Pupil).

is_head_of(jane,school).

part_of(class,school).
part_of(pupil,class).

is_a(roger,pupil).
is_a(john,teacher).

teaches(teacher,class).
```

The screen displayed when this program is run is shown in Fig. 14.4.

Fig 14.4

```
   Files        Edit         Run        Compile          Options      Setup
 ----------------Editor----------------                  -------------Dialog----
    Line 3    Col 1   B:SCHOOL3.PRO    Indent Insert    Goal: is_a_pupil_of_
 predicates                                             (Who,What)
                                                        Who=jane, What=roger
 is_head_of_(symbol,symbol)                             1 Solution
 part_of(symbol,symbol)                                 Goal: is_a_pupil_of_
 is_a(symbol,symbol)                                    (jane,What)
 teaches_maths_to(symbol,symbol)                        What=roger
 studies(symbol,symbol)                                 1 Solution
 specialises_in(symbol,symbol)                          Goal: is_a_pupil_of_
                                                        (Who,roger)
 clauses                                                Who=jane
                                                        1 Solution
 teaches_maths_to(Teachername,Pupilname) if             Goal:
 teaches(Teacher,Class)and
 -------------Message----------------                  -------------Trace-------
 is_a_pupil_of
 is_head_of
 is_a_pupil_of
 is_a
 --------------------------------------------------------------------------------
 F2-Save F3-Load F5-Zoom F6-Next F8-Previous goal Shift-F10-Resize F10-Goal
```

14.6 ANOTHER EXAMPLE

The example mentioned in section 14.3 regarding a program to help you decide about buying a car does not lend itself very well to being written in a language such as BASIC but can be written in PROLOG, as can be seen next. It may not be perfect in that there are no frills on the program to present it respectably. It is only the structure of the program and the use of the PROLOG language which is important at this stage.

```
predicates

            action(symbol)
            purchase(symbol)
            like_it(symbol)
            new_one(symbol)
            low_mile(symbol)
            one_own(symbol)
            good_cond(symbol)
            check_cond(symbol)
            trade_in(symbol)
            cash(symbol)
            hp(symbol)
            afford_it(symbol)

  clauses

            action(dont) if like_it(no),!.
            action(dont) if purchase(likely) and trade_in(bad),!.
            action(buy) if purchase(probable) and cash(available),!.
            action(dont) if check_cond(yes) and low_mile(no) or
            one_own(no) or good_cond(no),!.
            action(buy) if hp(possible) and afford_it(yes),!.
            action(dont) if hp(not_possible),!.
            action(dont) if afford_it(no),!.
            hp(possible) if purchase(probable) and cash(not_available),!.

            purchase(likely) if check_cond(yes) and one_own(yes) and
good_cond(yes).
            purchase(probable) if purchase(likely) and trade_in(good),!.
            purchase(possible) if like_it(yes),!.
            purchase(likely) if purchase(possible) and new_one(new),!.
            check_cond(yes) if purchase(possible) and new_one(old),!.
```

```
like_it(yes).
new_one(old).
low_mile(yes).
good_cond(yes).
cash(available).
afford_it(_).
one_own(no).
trade_in(good).
```

The blank in the brackets indicates that the object in irrelevant in this case. All the predicates must have some value for the program to work. In order to prevent PROLOG having to back-track over sections that do not need to be examined more than once the **cut** symbol, !, is placed at the end of a line which needs to be executed once only. The goal in this example would be

action(What)

14.7 A WORD OF WARNING

As you can see from this chapter, PROLOG is very good at doing what it is designed to do. But do not try to perform any complex calculations using this language. Although PROLOG programs can perform arithmetic, a program such as the electricity bill program featured in several parts of this book proves far more difficult to write than it appears at first sight. Which goes to demonstrate, as we said in the Preface, that choosing the right program is very much a "horses for courses" situation. An example of a PROLOG program to add a series of numbers up - a very short program when written in BASIC - is shown next. It seems to make the point!

```
/* Frank Hatfull BSc CS4
   29.10.88
   Prolog Ass 1  part A
   Get list of numbers, give totals
*/

%trace
predicates
    intro.
```

```prolog
    addnum(integer,integer).
    Validate(string,integer,integer).

goal
    intro(),
    Total = 0,
    Count = 0,
    addnum(Total,Count).

clauses

  /* intro message */
  intro() if
    write("    Enter Numbers to Add Up"),nl,
    write("           or Q to Quit"),nl.

  /* main loop - get and add up inputs */
  addnum(Total,Count) if
    write(".> "),                          % write prompt
    readln(NumString),                     % get input string
    validate(NumString,Num,Inc),!,         % return a valid number +
increment
    CurrTotal = Total + Num,               % sum current total
    write("   Current Total : ",CurrTotal),nl,
    CountTotal = Count + Inc,                % increment count for
averages
    addnum(CurrTotal,CountTotal).          % go through loop again

  /* catch after termination - print totals*/
  addnum(CurrTotal,Count) if
    Average = CurrTotal / Count,           % calculate average print
totals
    write("   Grand Total  : ",CurrTotal),nl,
    write("   Count        : ",Count)   ,nl,
    write("   Average      : ",Average) ,nl,
    fail.

  /* validate range  -  zero to 100  - is valid */
  validate(NumString,Num,Inc) if
    str_int(NumString,Num),                % convert input string to
numeric
    Num < 100 and Num >= 0,!,              % check range
    Inc = 1,                               % return incremental count

    true.

  /* Check for invalid character string */
```

```
   validate(NumString,Num,Inc) if
     str_len(NumString,Len),                % check input length
     Len > 1,                               % if over 1
     write(" [ ", NumString , " Invalid Value ]"),nl,
     Inc = 0,                               % return zero increment
     Num = 0,                               % return zero number
     true.

 /* Check for invalid character - NB Q is valid */
  validate(NumString,Num,Inc) if
     str_char(NumString,C),                    % convert string to
character
     C <> 'Q',                          % if not "Quit"
     write(" [ ", C , " Invalid Character ]"),nl,
     Inc = 0,                                  % return zero increment

     Num = 0,                               % return zero number
     true.

 /* check for blank return & do nothing */
  validate(NumString,Num,Inc) if
     str_len(NumString,Len),                % check input length
     Len = 0,                               % if just carriage return
     Inc = 0,                               % return zero increment
     Num = 0,                               % return zero number
     true.

 /* check for termination ie "Q" */
  validate(NumString,_,_) if
     str_char(NumString,C),                 % convert input to character

     C = 'Q',                               % if "Quit"
     write("   Terminated by user "),nl,
     fail.                                  % fail & drop out of main
loop

/* end  of program */
```

When the program is run the dialog looks like this:

```
        Enter Numbers to Add Up
           or Q to Quit
 .> 5
    Current Total : 5
 .> 6
   Current Total : 11
```

```
.> 12
   Current Total : 23
.> 101
[ 101 Invalid Value ]
   Current Total : 23
.> 67
   Current Total : 90
.> q
 [ q Invalid Character ]
   Current Total : 90
.> Q
   Terminated by user
   Grand Total  : 90
   Count        : 4
   Average      : 22.5
```

FURTHER READING

Boris Allen (1987) C Programming, Principals and Practice, Paradigm.

The Alvey Report : A programme for advanced Information. Technology (September 1982) HMSO.

Craig Bolon (1986) Mastering C, Sybex.

Peter Gosling (1981) Program your micro in BASIC, Macmillan.

Peter Gosling (1983) Practical BASIC Programming, Macmillan.

Peter Gosling (1989) Mastering Spreadsheets, Macmillan.

Peter Gosling (1989) Easily into dBASE III Plus, Macmillan.

Peter Gosling (1989) Easily into dBASE III Plus Programming, Macmillan.

Peter and Joanna Gosling (1988) Mastering Word Processing, Macmillan (2nd edn).

Eric Huggins (1983) Mastering Pascal Programming, Macmillan.

Roger Hutty (1983) Mastering COBOL Programming, Macmillan.

Edward Jones (1987) Using dBASE III Plus, Osborne McGraw-Hill.

Kernighan and Richie (1978) The C Programming Language, Prentice-Hall.

M. de Pace (1986) dBASE Programming Language, Collins.

Andrew Parkin (1982) COBOL for Students, Arnold.

Stephen Prata (1987) Advanced C Primer ++, Sams.

Elaine Rich (1988) Artificial Intelligence, McGraw-Hill.

Herbert Schildt (1986) Advanced Turbo Pascal, Osborne McGraw-Hill.

Douglas S. Stivison (1985) Introduction to Turbo Pascal, Sybex.

Bjarne Stroustrup (1988) C++, AT & T Bell Laboratories, Murray Hill.

Patrick Henry Winston (1984) Artificial Intelligence, Addison-Wesley (2nd edn).

G.G.L.Wright (1982) Mastering Computers, Macmillan.

INDEX